A HOME OF ONE'S OWN

ALSO BY HASHI MOHAMED

*People Like Us: What it Takes to
Make it in Modern Britain*

A HOME OF ONE'S OWN

HASHI MOHAMED

P

PROFILE BOOKS

First published in Great Britain in 2022 by
Profile Books Ltd
29 Cloth Fair
London
ECIA 7JQ

www.profilebooks.com

1 3 5 7 9 10 8 6 4 2

Typeset in Dante by MacGuru Ltd
Printed and bound in Great Britain by
CPI Group (UK) Ltd, Croydon, CRO 4YY

The moral right of the author has been asserted.

A CIP catalogue record for this book is
available from the British Library.

ISBN 978 1 80081 126 3
eISBN 978 1 80081 127 0

For the late Stephen Ashworth
and
my dear uncle Ardofe

INTRODUCTION

Above the North Wembley train station, in the London Borough of Brent, was a small three-bedroom flat where 18 people lived. This was the start of 1994, and I was one of the many children who belonged to the three households sharing this crowded space, waiting for the local council to do something about it.

Every other day, we would walk down Harrowdene Road as a group, usually headed by my sister, a mother of two in her early twenties, with my other three siblings in tow – all of us under the age of 12.

We would walk the journey of just over a mile partly on the main road, but the best bit was on a footpath parallel to the train tracks serving the London Underground and National

Rail trains on their way to Birmingham and Glasgow. It was always the most exciting part of the journey, which should have been a brisk 30 minutes but instead usually took more than an hour as we stopped frequently to gawp at the passing trains. On the way back it was an excellent result if we had not spent the entire day on this outing, and even better if sweets were in the offing as a reward for good behaviour.

Our little party was headed to Mahatma Gandhi House, the home of Brent Council's housing department, a stone's throw away from Wembley Stadium. This was the place where we spent so many years, throughout my childhood and teenage years, going back and forth to try to alleviate our housing situation. Because, although we always had a roof over our heads, my family was, in almost all senses of the word, homeless. But we did not know it, and we did not understand it as such. Looking back, I don't think we ever noticed the proximity to the famous national stadium: for us, Mahatma Gandhi House was by far the most important building in the area, the place where dreams were made and crushed.

When I arrived in Britain as a nine-year-old refugee boy, we were stateless, and without direction. We had escaped the civil war in Somalia and become displaced. We had lost our homeland and were without roots; we would remain without stability and without a secure roof for the next decade and a half. We lived in hugely crowded spaces, sharing one room to four, sometimes five of us. We were moved around from one squalid council accommodation to the next, never knowing when the next legal notice would be served to move us on to another property. Each time a term ended, my siblings and I were never certain whether we would ever see the friends we had made in the local school again.

This was our version of London in the mid 1990s, and it was a real crossroads: a city poised between the Thatcher years and the enormous investment in social projects that came with New Labour, and which would ultimately help to transform my own life. Some of it feels today like ancient history – Tamagotchis and Britney Spears as a young ingénue – but at the same time, my family's story could be a description of a situation in any other major capital or city in the early years of the twenty-first century. My focus in this book is the United Kingdom, where I grew up and still live. But the broader points could apply equally, in different ways, to many modern cities in the West as well as developing cities elsewhere. A home is a home is a home, everywhere: just as it always has been. But at the same time, we live in a period of unprecedented, unequally distributed wealth, when the status quo only serves a few, when for many of us a constant roof over your head cannot be guaranteed. When, yet again, children are arriving from a war zone, having lost the only homes they have ever known, and facing an unknown future.

In many ways, not much has changed since my family was being shunted from one substandard flat to another: even if you make it into the UK – something that is more challenging today than it has been for decades, and certainly more so than when my own family arrived – a home is not something that can be taken for granted. To state the obvious, for too many in Britain today, owning (or even renting) a decent home is a financial impossibility. In 2019, before the pandemic, 17 per cent of people nationwide were living in housing that is not considered 'decent' at all, with 'non-decent' defined as containing 'a serious and immediate risk to a person's health and safety'. In 1987, six years before we arrived in London, the newly elected Member of Parliament for Brent South, Paul Boateng, gave a description of the housing crisis in his new constituency:

> In the borough of Brent, which is seventh on the list of housing deprivation in Greater London, the position grows worse daily. More than 800 families are crammed into bed-and-breakfast accommodation, and there are 1,500 homeless families in all.

Today, 35 years later, by way of example, the average overall waiting time for a council house in Brent is currently 14 years, with over 20,000 people registered on the waiting list.

I am, however, one of the lucky ones (although, as so often, that word 'lucky' conceals many years of struggle). As I write this in 2022, I have been a homeowner for seven years. My 18-month-old son has his own bedroom, in a safe, warm, clean house where he may well spend the whole of his childhood. Today I am also, perhaps coincidentally, perhaps not, a planning lawyer working to improve housing supply and quality, and contribute meaningfully to the law and policy whose results we can see unfolding across the country. One of the main reasons that I was drawn to this area of the law was a principle best articulated by a judge, Lord Justice Lindblom, when he said that it 'seemed more about making things right in the future than undoing things that had gone wrong in the past'.

But regardless, I know what it feels like to be homeless, or for your housing to feel like the opposite of a sanctuary. The fact that my family are now mostly, though not entirely, in stable housing arrangements represents literally years of work, patience and sacrifice on our part. From the moment my family arrived in the UK, we faced a number of humiliating personal experiences, many of which we shared with our neighbours. The council officers who failed to express any sympathy with our predicament, with our lack of language skills to explain our concerns. The frustrations and indignity of waiting at the housing offices the whole day only to be told to return the following day. Dealing with the authorities was often nothing short of dehumanising, as was trying to exist in the rodent-infested properties they apparently considered decent housing for a family with young children. These constituted threats to our mental and physical health. But there were also other ways in which it narrowed our horizons and limited our options. A lack of privacy and personal space was one: three generations living on top of each other was very common in our corner of northwest London, Brent, and remains so to a great extent still.

We were part of the great lists of statistics that governments and councils and think tanks produce in order to better understand the 'housing problem'. But it also affected us in subtle, harder-to-quantify ways. For example, the cramped flat we were stuffed into seemed to limit our horizons not just physically but mentally: we suffered from a very real inability to imagine how things could be better, how any of us could get out of our situation and live the kind of life I now have. It affects your relationship with trust when you cannot rely on being able to see your teachers and friends the following week. When you constantly have to learn a new route to school, or have to visit a new corner shop whose shelves are stacked differently, you end up disorientated not just in space, but in your relationship to the world as a whole; where you fit into the society you live in. It seeps into your core, infecting your relationship with your surroundings, distorting your perception of reality, and completely transforming your understanding of institutions and what they're there to do.

I strongly believe that our lack of prospects more generally could be traced back to how we lived, for the absence of firm foundations do little to offer a future that is not built on sand. It is true that Brent – and many other inner-city areas in Britain – has improved enormously since we were visiting Mahatma Gandhi House. Relative poverty and more widespread deprivation has improved, employment (albeit much of it insecure) has gone up. The availability of advice, guidance and community action groups have all changed how we view poverty and how it affects life chances. Many of the local schools are unrecognisable today. But it is clear to me that without drastic changes in the availability of decent housing, and in particular affordable social housing, all other progress will be fundamentally undermined. We can continue to talk about the 'levelling up' of society all we want, but if we cannot guarantee our children a proper home they can call their own, we are setting them up for failure. We have failed to appreciate the significant divide that, in one of the richest countries in the world, exists among us in the most basic of human rights: a place that remains yours, not just for a night or a month but for a year, a decade, for as long as you want to stay.

Putting my son to bed in his quiet room every evening is a surprisingly profound experience for me. Because I also know what it feels like to have a home of my own, to have that sense of security, I know how that changes things too. How your mind is much more settled, allowing a state of calm to develop that naturally transfers into your daily activities, your routine and life choices. It allows the mind and soul to wander to more important matters; the growth of one's personality, the ability to dream and desire. It gives you gifts beyond warmth and shelter: things like focus, freedom, a sense of belonging, the ability to allow your life to unfold in a way that truly matters, rather than scrabbling from day to day. It allows you to turn your attention from daily survival to wider society as a whole, to change, to then leading a life that allows some kind of a legacy for you and your family.

None of this is really possible without a home to call one's own. This matters to me immensely; it matters because I have experienced it first hand and I am now working in an industry directly intertwined with the flawed system, attempting to improve on the dire situation. But also because I believe that we have allowed ourselves to be lulled into a sense of, if not exactly false security, then a misunderstanding of why the housing crisis matters – which I see as perhaps the most pressing issue of our time (second only to and related closely with climate change). It lies at the heart of a really significant number of issues we are facing at the moment. And it requires urgent attention.

A HOME OF ONE'S OWN

In this book, I want to define the problem generally known as 'the housing crisis' better, to
give it a personal expression, a professional
analysis, and to offer some solutions. Concerns around the quality of accommodation
have arguably always been around: in *Bleak
House* Charles Dickens wrote about London's
'tumbling tenements [that] contain, by night,
a swarm of misery'. More recently it was the
subject of Ken Loach's TV play *Cathy Come
Home* (1966), a documentary-style drama that
depicts so powerfully a young couple's desperate search for adequate housing in post-war
Britain. But if the root cause of the 'housing
crisis' has no directly definable origin, it
does relate to a concern that emerged most

prominently in the 1980s–90s, became more acute in the 2000s, and dominates headlines today. This particular housing crisis is marked above all by a gap between expectation and affordability, by generational tension, and by the difference in equality and equity between those who have and those who continue to struggle with no clear sight of a way out. All viewed against a context of a severe lack of available homes, reductions in affordability and compromised quality, and now a dramatic increase in the cost of living.

This book seeks to be a plea to policy makers and key decision takers – governments, local and national; those seeking to build homes; those already on the property ladder, and many more – to think better. To think again about the distribution of homes, and about what home ownership means generally, but also specifically in terms of secure and genuinely affordable renting; to see the housing crisis as not just a knotty policy problem, a complicated and dull tangle of think tanks, pressure groups, competing needs and contradictory legal frameworks, but as a fundamental issue of justice that underpins and exasperates a vast number of other injustices in our society today. Crucially, to not think about houses in the abstract sense, but about homes for the people who need them most: those for whom home is not something to be taken for granted. Those who desperately need us all to find a solution, and to radically change our perspectives.

But most of all, it is for all of us who have struggled to find – and hold on to – a home of our own. It is a statement of solidarity, a reassurance that the situation in which we find ourselves is neither fair nor normal, and that it can change for the better. And it is a reminder that, even when our own circumstances change for the better, it remains our collective responsibility to change things for society as a whole. The title of this book is inspired by Virginia Woolf's extended essay *A Room of One's Own*, first published in September 1929. In it, Woolf explores how the social injustices of both her own time, and more generally through history, have prevented women from being able to write, explore their own ideas and develop intellectually as their male counterparts have done. Central to this analysis was her much-quoted observation that 'a woman must have money and a room of her own if she is to write fiction'. Woolf's contention is ultimately that space – private, secure, quiet space – is essential for an individual to thrive and reach their fullest potential. This is why I am interested in it. It is personal to me and so many people like me, who did not have that space available to them.

I wish to take this idea further – in ways that Woolf herself raises – and apply it to one of this century's most pressing problems: the lack of housing, and in particular affordable housing in places where there are opportunities and where people wish to live. Woolf was interested not just in the lack of a quiet, private space itself, but also more generally in the kinds of spaces that were not open to women, and what it means to be shut out of, for example, a library or an Oxford college, places which are engineered specifically to create opportunities for intellectual development and exchange.

There's an interplay between not just the intellect and place, but the kinds of personalities that are allowed to develop within it: 'the urbanity, the geniality, the dignity which are the offspring of luxury and privacy and space'.

The strength of *A Room of One's Own* is partly found in the way it makes something vague and general – a lack of representation and opportunities, the absence of women from the intellectual discourse of their day – personal and particular. Woolf was concerned about how the absence of something concrete – a room, the financial means for independence – was distorting literature itself, using the example of what would have happened had 'Shakespeare had a wonderfully gifted sister, called Judith'. Judith, it might not surprise you to learn, does not become the most famous English-language playwright of all time, but instead ends up buried in an unmarked grave, her plays unwritten and her voice silenced. By extension, Woolf draws out what we have lost through centuries of starving women of the opportunity to create work on a par with their male peers. As I have said, there's a temptation today to see the housing crisis as something too big, too complicated and too intractable to wrestle with ourselves – we're not sure whether it's a social issue, a legal one, a political one, an economic problem, or even a humanitarian one. But fundamentally, it's an issue of loss – what we lose individually, in terms of opportunities to grow, learn, experiment, consider and rest, and what we lose more generally in terms of talent, potential, health, time, happiness and opportunities, if we fail to provide the most basic of resources to our citizens.

Nowhere to go

Before we explore these ideas further, we should start with both where we are now and, just as importantly, how we got here; most significantly, how the apparently relatively robust and well-resourced housing sector of the 1950s and 1960s became the obstinate ruin it is today. It will be impossible to cover in such a short book the comprehensive kaleidoscope of issues and arguments in this area; this is

not, you will be relieved to hear, meant to be
a policy document dissecting each and every
failure, nor a rewriting of the legal framework or an attempt to recast afresh the policy
prescriptions or political history. While I will
attempt to offer some solutions, this book is
really about *why* all this matters. It is about the
underlying issues whose tentacles are flowing
through to the rest of society; their effect on
education, on health and wellbeing, on opportunities and family life, on the future prospects
and present predicaments.

There has perhaps never truly been a 'golden
age' of housing in Britain, and each successive decade has piled up both innovations and
regressions. Dickens, quoted earlier, talked
about 'ruined shelters [that] have bred a crowd
of foul existence that crawls in and out of
gaps in walls and boards … sowing more evil
in its every footprint than Lord Coodle, and
Sir Thomas Doodle, and the Duke of Foodle,
and all the fine gentlemen in office, down to
Zoodle, shall set right in five hundred years

– though born expressly to do it'. It's a criticism of the housing crisis that still rings true today: the out-of-touch ruling class are hopelessly inadequate to deal with the entrenched inequality and misery on the ground. In 1862, around a decade later, George Peabody, a banker and philanthropist who was part of the circle of reformers that also included Dickens, would found the first of the capital's Peabody Estates, providing decent housing for the poor. Innovative and far-sighted as they were for the time, the Peabody Estates also had rigid 'moral' standards: residents were subject to a curfew and strict rules for behaviour – like the housing provided by the Quaker businessmen and philanthropists Joseph Rowntree and Richard Cadbury, it was both a way of providing for the poor or working class, but also offered an opportunity to control or perhaps, as the Victorians would have thought of it, 'improve' them.

Housing quality would remain an issue well into the twentieth century: it wouldn't be until after the First World War, with the 1919 Housing Act, that subsidies would be provided to build council housing, ostensibly to provide 'a land fit for heroes'. At the time, 80 per cent of people were in the private rental sector, and council housing offered a new opportunity for decent, stable homes. The middle part of the century would be dominated by large, ambitious housing initiatives and building projects: in the 35 years following the end of the Second World War, local authorities and housing associations built 4.4 million of what we might today call social homes. In the 1950s, under a Conservative government, 182,242 local authority houses were being built a year on average during the decade; by 1968, the total number of houses being built annually was a little over 350,000 dwellings. By 1979, a staggering 32 per cent of Britons lived in council accommodation, compared to today, where the number hovers around 8 per cent. But it wasn't all sunshine and roses: only around the late 1960s was house building equal to demand, and the 1970s were marked by financial crises and inflation that made it difficult for people to get on the housing ladder.

But 1979 was also the year that Margaret Thatcher was elected, an event that is absolutely crucial to understanding how we have reached the situation in which we find ourselves today. The 'Right to Buy' policy introduced in the Housing Act of 1980 allowed council tenants to purchase their home at significant discounts, homes that then made their way into the privately rented market, often with the same councils now renting them to house tenants. This was also the natural consequence of the collapse in supply, rather than just the transfer of ownership of one individual unit. The homes sold off via the Right to Buy scheme were never replaced in the same quantities, and the real-world consequence of this significant change introduced in the 1980s by the Thatcher government is one of the core reasons we find ourselves living through a housing 'crisis'. (It is important to acknowledge that much of the council housing stock was not the best quality, and that this particular policy was also at the time hugely popular, seen as a way of building a property-owning democracy giving hope to many.) At the same time, the amount of housing being built began to decline: in 1980, 88,530 homes were built by councils. By 1983, just three years later, the supply had more than halved to just 39,170. In 2019, 6,287 new council homes were delivered. Currently, nationwide, there are 1.1 million people across the country on the waiting list, and as of 2020/21, 136 of 314 local authorities do not own or control any dwellings.

The time when I was growing up, the 1990s, marked a huge change not just in the UK, but globally: the Berlin Wall had fallen, the internet was on the rise, footballers stopped being sportsmen and became multi-millionaires. We had 'Wonderwall' and Lady Di. And after almost two decades of Conservative rule, we suddenly had New Labour. It was also the beginning of imminent significant financial injection into public services, which would all go on to transform how we lived and interacted. And yet what was missing was a strategic understanding of where the housing market was headed, and how various policy decisions (or indecision) were likely to just exacerbate the present situation. The architects of New Labour poured funds into schools and public services, but never seemed to appreciate the role that a well-regulated housing market – at the time, quickly running out of control – plays in social issues, from health to social mobility.

While all of this was going on, significant social and economic changes were underway. Britain's population grew from just over 56 million in 1979 to nearly 67 million today, with migration being the main driver of the UK's population since the 1990s. We began to live longer, and our population is now, on average, older. By this point manufacturing had significantly declined; many factories and coal mines had closed as Thatcher sought to reimagine Britain's place in an increasingly global and globalised world.

Our economy became overly dependent on the services industry, namely the financial sector, legal services, accounting and auditing services, consultancies and IT, currently representing 80 per cent of total UK economic output. Society began shifting to professional jobs requiring more formal qualifications, with more emphasis on higher-paid city jobs and much less on well-paid, traditionally working-class jobs. The disparity between what a banker or a footballer would be paid compared to a nurse or police officer starkly represented the new divide, and opportunities to re-train became non-existent. Whole towns and villages have been left with the scars of booming yesteryears, and many of our citizens cannot afford to live in the society we have now built. Meanwhile, house prices have risen exponentially, pushing more and more people into the unaffordable private rental sector: in 2021, the Office for National Statistics released figures that reveal quite how fast this is moving, saying 'we estimate that full-time employees could typically expect to spend around 9.1 times their workplace-based annual earnings on purchasing a home in England. This is a statistically significant increase compared with 2020, when it was 7.9 times their workplace-based annual earnings.'

This whole changing context has consequences for the taxpayer: in 2018–19, the Office
for Budget Responsibility estimated that
housing benefit spending (the money that the
government pays to people who cannot afford
to pay their rents) rose to £23.4 billion, 2.9 per
cent of total public spending. In human terms,
this is a million families paying rents they
cannot afford, leaving nine in ten of these families in poverty. Working, or even working hard,
is not necessarily the answer either: the Joseph
Rowntree Foundation found 748,000 families
could not afford their rent with one or more
adults in work, two-thirds of whom work full-
time. Neither is leaving the crowded, expensive
cities: contrary to the common misconception,
high rents (in relation to local affordability) are
not an exclusive property of London, Hong
Kong, New York, Toronto or Paris – some of
the effects are felt just as acutely in Cornwall,
Essex and Wales, although the so-called 'after
housing costs' poverty rates are the highest
in London. In short, the chronic problem of
some section of the population being unable

to pay market prices for renting or purchase is found across the country, even if its severity is not evenly distributed.

In essence, we have a perverse situation in which there has been an enormous decline in social housing stock, mainly due to the government's decision to sell off homes without replacing them. This persisted through successive governments: Labour, Coalition and Conservative. Concurrently, we have seen an increase in the population and therefore naturally a rise in people who need housing. The economy within which we are all expected to make a living has completely transformed – and society, our education system, successive government and policy makers have all missed the opportunity to prepare us for that transformation, particularly in a way that could have meant us competing in various industries, not least the technological revolution, the ability to learn multiple languages, and just new skills for an unrecognisable twenty-first-century working environment. People whose wages have simply not kept up with rapidly rising house prices have been pushed into often inadequate and insecure tenancies in the private sector, where their basic need for shelter has become an income for those who have been able to get on the housing ladder. The government only reappears in the picture to subsidise the privately rented sector through welfare spending, funded by the taxpayer.

Belatedly, there has been a recognition of this being a problem: the taxes on second homes changing, mortgage interest no longer being a tax-deductible expense (which fully came into effect in April 2020 following a phasing period from 2017), and the additional stamp duty payable on second homes. But these measures are so obvious that one wonders why it took so long to get a grip. Where they have intervened to encourage more house building, it has not been enough nor fast enough to keep up. Policy interventions such as 'Help to Buy' (essentially government underwriting some mortgages) or the stamp duty holiday have all contributed to boosting the demand in the property market without fundamentally grappling with the question of limited supply. This has had a direct and demonstrable impact on increasing property prices, meaning the rich get richer without doing anything, and the poor get poorer through no fault of their own.

Housing is today seen as a precious asset class: land value rises significantly once it has the benefit of planning permission. This is a fundamental failure of policy. Like a number of public problems (NHS waiting lists, adult social care, education), what we have is a situation where there are strong feelings, but poor popular understanding of the underlying symptoms and potential solutions. Naturally it means that things then get worse year on year, and there are objective rational reasons for why it is difficult to find a simple, quick solution. Housing speaks to something deeply embedded in British culture, which makes it such a polarising issue, in which clear high stakes for so many vested interests are often pitted against communities who understand there is a significant problem, but also see their own properties as their proudest lifetime achievement, and largest personal asset. You could not have designed a more insane situation if you tried.

Why does all this matter?

If today a home to call one's own is one of the most important foundations for anyone seeking personal advancement, security and a stable future, it is unfortunately one that has, for many of us, become an unattainable goal: as home ownership dwindles and council housing depletes, more and more of us are caught in insecure tenancies, at worst at risk of eviction and at best unable to truly call our home our own.

Owning a home isn't the be-all-and-end-all solution to housing, and in other parts of the world like Germany and Scandinavia – where long-term renting is more the norm, and renters thus have better legal protections – people are often bemused by the British obsession with home ownership. But it makes sense, in a country where tenancies tend to be short term and rents volatile, and tenants have limited rights to, for example, change their homes to suit them better – as anyone who has ever had to send three emails to get permission to put in a nail to hang a picture can attest to. Home ownership gives you (in theory) a valuable asset with more staying power than your dwindling pension pot, a bulwark against having to rent in old age, and an opportunity to live with wallpaper you chose yourself. That last point seems like the least important but can have an enormous emotional impact, especially if your life is otherwise dictated by forces outside your control: one of the most formative moments of my childhood was when my primary school teacher allowed us to redecorate our classroom in the school holidays, using paint and design we'd chosen ourselves.

Though the Office for National Statistics' calculation that a person in full-time employment would typically need to spend over nine times their annual salary on purchasing a home, most mortgage lenders cap borrowing at 4.5 or 5 times your salary. These ratios become even wider in major cities around the country, where incidentally the best jobs and opportunities happen to be clustered.

The volatility in the interest rates in the 1970s through to the 1990s might not have been desirable, but it allowed for some movement in a climate of high risk and high reward. In December 2021, the Resolution Foundation, the think tank focused on looking at trends around living standards in Britain, released findings on the decline of home ownership in the age bracket 25–34, which stands at 28 per cent across the board, but among the poorest two-fifths of society stands at just 11 per cent (comparatively, in 1989 the figures were 51 per cent and 24 per cent).

And the problems faced in property ownership cannot be seen exclusively as a matter of just the supply and demand of housing, although that is part of the problem. It is also fundamentally about the kind of economies we have allowed to establish, the kind of markets that work in favour of a lucky minority. This is something which I have only come to truly appreciate as a barrister specialising in planning and environment law, although my eyes were further opened when I met a bank manager who said I would not have a problem getting a mortgage because banks see 'barristers as a safe bet'. When I interviewed Dr Deborah Potts, the Emeritus Reader in Human Geography at King's College London, and author of *Broken Cities*, for a Radio 4 documentary on the housing crisis, I was struck by her point that in order to understand the situation, it is critical to appreciate that the people seeking to establish homes are embedded in fundamentally skewed labour markets, where the price of one's labour is determined by market conditions. What this ultimately means is that there are millions of people in work who will never, by themselves, earn sufficient income to either live in decent legal housing, or convince a bank to lend to them. This includes multiple members of my family who work public sector jobs: bus drivers, those serving in the NHS, teachers and so on. It is, frankly, a rigged system; one which expects new entrants to work for decades in order to get to the point where they can meet the ever-moving deposit thresholds. And unless you're living at home rent free for a number of years in order to save up, your income will predominantly go to meeting rent and living expenses.

The issue is fundamentally about the lack of affordability for those who want to buy but don't earn enough. And then there is the poor quality of homes with no security of tenure for those who cannot buy. The two are linked and there is no third option. Of course, as I will go on to discuss, ownership by itself isn't the answer to this crisis, but the demand for more housing has grown unabated, and if young people can't buy or access council housing, the reality is that they will now spend a significant chunk of their monthly incomes on rent. And what then makes the situation quite perverse is not only the poor quality of privately rented accommodation in many places, but that it is comparatively more expensive than a mortgage and socially rented housing of all types. Unsurprisingly, more and more young people at the start of their lives or careers are now living in uncertain, unsustainable and unstable accommodation, situations that may continue into their thirties or even longer. This lack of control over something as essential as where you live – and who you live with – then ends up setting the tone for the beginning of their adult lives. Indeed, it may set the tone for their old age as well: while today most pensioners own their own homes, the ONS estimates that far more millennials will enter old age – with all the insecurity that entails – still in the private rental sector.

Meanwhile young people lamenting this state of affairs are unfairly caricatured as a spoilt generation spending their savings on avocados and Netflix subscriptions, which is both insulting and disingenuous. Returning to the figures collected by the Resolution Foundation, it seems that the vast majority of young renters (73 per cent) would prefer to own their homes, given the opportunity. But their chances of doing so have fallen not just as a whole, but especially sharply among specific groups: rates of home ownership among the poorest two-thirds of young people have fallen much more sharply than their better-off counterparts. Almost half (48 per cent) of young families that don't own their own home have less than £1,000 in savings. Yes, it was difficult to get a mortgage 20 or 30 years ago, but at least the average house price was not completely on a different planet to the average salary.

Today, again, without the extra assistance of the bank of mum and dad, or the advantage that comes with buying property with a joint income, only a minority within a minority can achieve home ownership. If you take the housing association property where my mother and some of my siblings live, she waited over a decade to be securely housed. This property is now worth close to £500,000, and there is absolutely no possibility that any of my siblings will get a mortgage to be able to buy, and renting at full market prices would make it almost affordable for three working adults with no time for any other thing but work. As I was putting the finishing touches to this manuscript in May 2022, Boris Johnson's struggling premiership had just announced plans to extend Right to Buy to include housing association renters – a populist promise that is completely unworkable in practice, but also fails to fully appreciate the lessons from the very recent past.

Today, interest rates have been kept artificially low for almost a decade and a half, which has been to the benefit of those enjoying the status quo. A change in these rates by a few percentage points could prove calamitous for many homeowners and prospective homeowners, creating instability for the banks and those to whom they have lent in the past. The capital appreciation in properties was also aided by quantitative easing policy by the bank, an indirect monetary tool of essentially printing money (started by the outgoing Labour government and subsequently maintained) following the financial crisis of 2008. This pumping of cash into the economy inevitably feeds into house prices, which only helps those that have as opposed to those who do not: the carefully engineered stability today protects those on the ladder (and the few who are able to join) at the expense of everyone else.

All of this, to me, shows how we have become fixated with the housing crisis as a problem of supply and demand, of market forces, when its roots run much deeper than that. It doesn't matter how much housing is available to buy or rent if you only have £1,000 in the bank; it doesn't even matter how much 'affordable' housing is available if the definition of affordable is completely out of kilter with what most people can afford. It is a market problem – but it is a problem of the economic market we are all being asked to participate in, in which many people are increasingly trapped in low-paid and insecure work while paying high rents and with no opportunity to escape from the cycle.

Some of the Scandinavian nations, Britain and China have all sought to create housing supply rented at rates that have absolutely nothing to do with market value. This is what we call the social rented sector, essentially highly subsidised private rentals – in Britain this is usually managed by a local authority or a housing association. This is the only way that it is currently achievable, which means that when the state seeks to provide housing for the homeless in the private sector (because its own stock is at capacity), it often leads to the state subsidising the rent and thereby effectively contributing to or paying a private individual's mortgage. Is this the only real way to address this problem?

I have become more and more convinced that fixing the situation will require government intervention on an enormous scale, something that has been absent for the best part of 40 years. The issue we face is quite simple: the legacy of a highly productive post-war boom, followed by the highly unstable 1970s aftermath, in turn ushering in Margaret Thatcher's liberalisation policies and the stubborn delusion that less government intervention and more market competition is the only way to salvation. Most people, of whatever political persuasion, will readily accept that the current situation is a classic example of market failure. It is time to think again.

I am not proposing some socialist utopia, an ideal that has never existed. What I am talking about are policies, regulation and government interventions that have successfully worked, followed by Conservative and Labour governments alike, and which would not necessarily seek to discourage the contributions of market forces to our housing market. What we need is more social housing owned and secured for the benefit of those who are shut out of the market, who may never achieve ownership in their own lifetime, but who deserve to live better than they do now and to have options beyond the private rental sector. The way we once did it was to try to give millions access to good-quality (not always the case in practice), secure homes and the dignity that came with it. And with that dignity, other opportunities too – space to be happy and flourish, space to grow, think and seize opportunities for themselves and their families. This huge need for genuinely affordable social housing, which can only be met realistically via government intervention, is entirely urgent.

*

One of the things about poor housing is that it amplifies – and is itself amplified – by any other problem you might be facing. Living in inadequate housing is stressful, in a way that puts pressure on your physical and emotional health, and also on your relationships. This was the case for us growing up: school was a real respite for us and the adults looking after us. It was seven hours, five times a week, in which we could escape somewhere else. Where we could learn but also explore in spaces which – although not beautiful or well-resourced by any means – were much better suited to our development than what we had at home.

In the past two years, during which we have been periodically forced to stay at home during a global pandemic, and our homes have also become our offices, we have spent more time there than we have ever done in modern times, making this conversation even more pertinent. The impact of the absence of educational infrastructure and framework, once seen as a great equaliser, an alternative place for many to find ways of transforming their lives, has been obvious. In particular, we have seen how those living in crowded homes, sharing bedrooms and laptops, without access to quiet spaces have fallen behind in their educational progress. We have seen those who have access to a garden, green spaces, or a place for children to play do better than those in tower blocks or in crowded inner cities, whose mental health has declined. They have been unable to benefit in the way that others have; through no fault of their own they have seen how their circumstances – already dire in some cases – have worsened even further. The true impact of all this we are still yet to fully appreciate; but it also made me realise how little some of us understand about how others in our own area live. I watched as people complained about teenagers 'hanging about in the park', when they'd been locked in with their parents, younger siblings and grandparents for months. I was interested to note who disappeared to a previously unmentioned second home in the country, appearing on Zoom from the walled garden. And I heard the inevitable dog-whistle comments about how the virus was spreading among 'certain communities' (often those who – either from choice or circumstances – live together in multi-generational families).

There is not a single city in the world today, a city that is growing and in which people (particularly the young) want to live, that is *not* suffering from a major housing/affordable-housing shortage. We have just had a stark reminder, in the form of a global crisis that forced us back into our homes, while also allowing us, via Zoom, a window into how others live. What does this do to our collective social contract? And how much longer can we sustain a crisis that is as much about deliberate design as it is about the law of unintended consequences?

An inheritance of loss

An odd function of the housing crisis is the sheer range of problems it covers: in one extreme, we have private landlords who own multiple properties and oligarchs stashing cash in lavish Central London homes, and at the other, we have people who don't have a home at all. The charity Crisis estimates, in England alone, that there are over 200,000 households experiencing the worst form of homelessness, which includes 'rough sleeping, people living in sheds, garages and other unconventional buildings, sofa surfing, hostels and unsuitable temporary accommodation such as B&Bs', with the figure being 219,000 at the end of 2019, prior to the exacerbating effect of the Covid-19 pandemic. And Britain is far from the only developed country in which people live in these conditions: Canada estimates that as many as 300,000 individuals experience homelessness, and in the USA the figure is over half a million.

There's sometimes a temptation to reduce the concept of shelter to having a 'roof over your head' – and that as long as you have *somewhere* to stay, then the problem is solved. But homelessness is more complex than that: the legal, statutory definition of homelessness is found in the Housing Act of 1996, which states first of all that 'a person is homeless if he has no accommodation available for his occupation', but goes on to point out that even if you have accommodation, you can still be considered homeless if that accommodation is threatened in any way – whether because you can't enter it, or a valid notice to vacate or a court order of eviction has been served or threatened. Sleeping rough might be almost unbelievably difficult and harmful (the mean age of death of a woman sleeping rough is 43, and of a man, 45), but this kind of housing precariousness, of juggling constantly between different options, never sure where you'll be sleeping next week, is terrible too.

Homelessness of every kind is not only an invisible barrier blocking people from attempting to reach new and better heights, it is also stifling the very conditions that normally make this possible. Not having a fixed abode or a consistent place to live in your most formative years disrupts your development as an individual, diverting energy that might otherwise be spent on thinking about what life offers.

This was certainly my experience growing up. I don't remember ever really thinking about what kind of future I could aspire to have, or what my options were in terms of work, university or travelling experiences. I do remember, though, thinking that it didn't matter that a doorknob was broken, or that the toilet flooded, or that this particular house was a longer distance from the nearest bus stop. It didn't matter because we'd move on next week, or next month, to a new location where we'd have to deal with another constellation of problems and concerns.

This is such a wearing and limiting way to view your life, your surroundings and your prospects. Of course, I didn't really see it that way all the time; for me, coming from a nomadic tradition, the constant movement was part of life. It was what our parents and grandparents did all the time. The challenge was how quickly you adapted, how quickly you settled into a new environment. But looking back, it was a source of trauma for all of us; this is not a way to have a decent start in the UK. This is not how one should be forced to approach life and all its possibilities. This is not what I would wish for my own child, that abiding sense of hopelessness that in adulthood has left me with a constant nagging sense of existential anxiety, an obsession with making sure I am secure in all senses. This is about every child having a wall on which they can stick a picture of a pop star or a football player, or just their own drawings, without wondering whether they should even bother.

The helplessness that comes with not having control over the most central, significant aspect of your life casts a shadow over the whole family. If the children feel hopeless, renting the space in their head to anxiety and fear, it also affects the parents, who often feel helpless because they can work every hour that God sends, only to not have much left after they have settled their bills.

In February 2022, the cost of living hit crisis point. The Bank of England's latest forecasts show a staggering inflation rise of over 7 per cent, with household incomes set to fall an average of £1,000 by the end of 2022, on the back of a sustained real-terms wage freeze since 2008. Energy prices have not risen this fast over the past 20 years, and many families will have to make genuine choices between putting food on the table and paying soaring bills and meeting their rents. This kind of poverty – I know all too well – takes up an enormous amount of time and emotional space. How will someone like this realistically save up a rental deposit on a bigger flat or fight off rent increases when tenancies are due for renewal? As we recover from the pandemic, and face an unprecedented cost-of-living crisis, we are now faced with a generation of children whose education has been disrupted, whose hopes are being stifled, and whose parents are struggling to meet their financial obligations, let alone provide the emotional support that those same children require to face life in the 2020s. It means many will be working, if at all possible, simply to sustain a living in an environment that is actually detrimental to one's full potential, to one's own health, sometimes lacking any real hope and oftentimes with no tangible way out. We understand, for instance, the clear relationship between damp and mould growth in the home and living conditions, and the adverse impact on health, particularly on children's developing lungs; but the way in which living in a cold, squalid home affects your mental health and mindset as a child feels much less tangible to us.

The psychotherapist Julia Samuel's book *Every Family Has a Story: How We Inherit Love and Loss* focuses on how the 'unresolved stressors of one generation can be passed down to intensify the daily pressures of life for the next'. In the collection of eight family narratives, she explains how relationships fundamentally influence our health and happiness – 'where we love and care most, we also hurt most' – and family is the only relationship that we cannot fully leave, however much we might try. A lack of access to good-quality, stable housing often leads to tension and conflict in the home. It can mean a loss of control, perhaps a loss of respect for one another too. It can damage relationships between generations, between siblings and extended relatives.

It may have long-lasting consequences to personal and family health – sometimes beyond the current generation, as Samuel explains. Just as wealthier families are able to pass down housing security to their children, the kind of trauma that comes with precarious housing arrangements can act almost like some kind of inter-generational undiagnosed post-traumatic stress disorder. It manifests itself in ways we are unable to fully appreciate in the here and now. It impacts us in multiple ways which are beyond our comprehension. Like how we might approach relationships, friendships, education, work and life at large. How we might approach the raising of our own children, what kind of life ambition we see for ourselves, or anger management and the various ways that this baggage might manifest itself in our minds and daily lives. Again, this speaks to the complete waste of potential, the complete failure of a society to harness each and every human's ability to make something of themselves and crucially then offer something to their society.

Many immigrant families, including my own, live with three generations under the same roof. Sometimes it can be by choice, but often it is because the younger generation cannot afford to move out, or have to wait much later to take the crucial step of finding their own place. Incidentally, the current dire situation means that this has become a wider issue for families with no recent immigrant history: cue headlines about 'boomerang kids' who return after university to live with their parents. Research carried out by Loughborough University suggests that the proportion of single, child-free 20–34-year-olds living with their parents went up 55 per cent between 2008 and 2017. In some cases, children marry but remain at home with their new spouses. Sometimes this is a choice, and in those cases the situation may work better, but often it is not voluntary and it can have a significant distorting effect on the personal growth of individuals and the dynamics within families: tensions over shared resources, sometimes anger over compromises that have to be made, a sense of guilt or even selfishness at the thought of wanting to leave and build your own space and sanctuary. And it is the same for the older generation who may also lack the resources that would allow them to live independently. A sense that they are a burden might take hold for those who are unable to take care of themselves, or are perhaps unable to afford – or are too scared – to live in a care home.

It seems to me, therefore, that a new social contract is needed. My generation, millennials, came of age in the post-2008 financial crisis, swiftly followed by major uncertainty in the workplace, rising personal debt, stagnating wages, Brexit, a global pandemic, a huge rise in the cost of living and now a rising threat of nuclear war that hasn't been seen since the previous century. As if this was not enough, they face three sets of costs that it is difficult to envisage a single generation being able to overcome or accommodate: the debts from higher education, a housing crisis and pension costs. And so the education they gain is more expensive than ever before, and it does not necessarily guarantee a way out of the current predicament. Home ownership is now out of reach for so many under the age of 40 without significant assistance (millennials are only half as likely to own their own home by the age of 30 as their parents), and not only are we now expected to work into our old age, the quality of that retirement, once accessed, is not guaranteed.

Home ownership is often discussed in terms of giving people a 'stake in society', but the converse is also the case: the lack of a fixed address is an absolute disaster if you want to play any sort of role in society at all. Something as simple as being able to receive a letter cuts out millions of people from being able to access basic rights as citizens: a staggering 14 per cent of UK adults have been unable to receive their post at some point over the last decade. Nearly 12 per cent of people have been unable to apply for services like health appointments, welfare benefits, bank accounts and even employment because they lack an address to put on applications. These figures become worse when you're disabled (24 per cent) or BAME (29 per cent). This was such a serious problem for my family growing up that we used to take it in turns as kids to revisit our old addresses at least once every couple of months, to ask whether any important mail had been delivered. It was completely unbearable – a brilliant example of how housing instability wastes your time and takes up mental space – and at times it was dangerous. We'd miss hospital appointments or specialist referrals because we didn't receive the letter.

There are *millions* of people at risk of being left behind by society without this most basic necessity, which would allow them to have some sort of contact and relationship with the institutional bodies that govern all our daily lives. This can mean no bank account, no driving licence, no passport, no GP surgery, no proof of address for an employer to contact you. Nowhere to recognise that you even exist. These are people effectively functioning outside of the framework of society as we understand it, with a slim chance of changing this. The toll on physical and mental health means that these are potentially productive people being completely severed from society, and again often through no fault of their own.

There are of course degrees of homelessness. There are those who face acute difficulties and those who live in varying degrees of unstable conditions. But they all share a common symptom, which is an attempt to live life in an environment where hopelessness and homelessness go hand in hand. A world where dreaming is impossible because a safe place to sleep is never guaranteed. And ultimately children and young people whose potential will never be truly unleashed through no fault of their own.

An issue of injustice

In 2018 I attended a conference to discuss housing and planning matters, addressed by Kit Malthouse, the then Minister of State for Housing and Planning (July 2018–July 2019).

He began his remarks by quipping that he was the minister in charge of solving the housing crisis … for now. It might have been a good joke, if behind it didn't lie a devastatingly serious point. In the past three decades, there has been more stability in the England football manager role than the position of the housing and planning minister. We have had 20 housing ministers since 1997, and 12 since 2010. It is hard to imagine another ministerial post that has been the victim of this much instability (apart from, perhaps, foreign secretary, of whom we have had five in six years). Every time an election rolls around, there is ample lip service paid by successive governments, metropolitan mayors, opposition parties and local councillors to the so-called 'housing crisis'. And yet, formulation of meaningful policy that has successfully confronted the crisis, or curtailed the ongoing increase in unaffordability, never seems to happen.

For me, the fact that we have not had a minister for housing in situ long enough to either actually grasp the complicated and highly technical landscape of housing policy, or to formulate ideas and policies that they then have the time to see through, speaks volumes about how serious we are about addressing this problem. Having said this, it would also seem that neither the civil servants nor the building industry seem to know how best to solve this issue either. The reality is that the housing brief is in many ways a poisoned chalice, a politically toxic problem that no one can bring themselves to address seriously, partly due to fear of alienating one constituency over another. The result is ministers merely holding things down until they can move somewhere more glamorous, more prestigious or less wrapped in complicated policy and regulations.

This stagnation and lack of political will is also fundamentally about the power structures in our society; namely that the ruling class, those who have the power to change the status quo (a minister in charge of housing, for example) do not see any political reason to change matters, nor indeed are they likely to disrupt that which directly and indirectly benefits them and their voters. It is one of the principal reasons why we get platitudes and jokes at conferences instead of serious and life-changing policy implemented today for the benefit of the next generation and beyond. Perhaps the ministerial revolving door is not the core cause; it is also true that part of the reason is that those with the power to change matters are the direct beneficiaries of the current system, and those who are yet to get on the property ladder similarly see themselves as potential future winners in a broken system. Let's be frank: this is a reality that even I am in multiple ways a beneficiary of.

If I was being generous, I would also say that housing ministers are caught between promises made to secure power that are fundamentally irreconcilable – namely, for example, to protect the green belt and green fields more generally – and to boost home ownership for all who wish to achieve it. These two basic positions cannot sit together, and no one in power with the ability to change matters has come forward to say this explicitly.

How have we tolerated today's lack of progress? It should be considered scandalous, but for some reason it remains under the radar, bubbling along while other crises dominate the headlines. But this political failure to properly grapple with one of the most serious issues of our time is affecting the lives and livelihoods of many of our citizens in real time. It is slowing down the system that is meant to provide and regulate housing, and confusing those working within it along the way. It is making us, en masse, completely cynical. It shows the cavalier attitude that persists in our political discourse around how life-changing decisions about our homes, environments and communities are approached by governments of all colours and stripes. We are all victims of a complete lack of vision and strategy. Generations have been let down by governments who have completely failed to appreciate all that flows from this crisis, to the detriment of the individual, the family, and society as a whole.

To have politicians over many years leave so many people living in conditions that they would not dream of occupying themselves is an unfortunate demonstration of the malaise at the heart of our democracy. That our leaders have not addressed meaningfully the persistent and widespread feeling of being unconnected with society, something that they mostly have been privileged not to experience, and if they had would certainly aim to do all that's possible to avoid it later in life, is damning. That feeling of not having your own personal space – the space to practise an instrument or read a book in peace; the sort of privacy that would allow you to enjoy your own silence and presence, knowing that, when asleep, no one will come in and turn on the light, waking you up – is a feeling I can still summon up today. How does none of this move or trouble those with the power to solve it? What does political leadership amount to if it does not do its bit to make this picture a reality for the majority of its citizens? Why do we elect governments if they do not present us with a vision that takes us to a place better than where they found us?

The total lack of leadership surrounding

fair distribution of resources is not even the most shocking part of all this. Whether in New York, Paris or, as with Grenfell Tower, in London, we have seen how the disparities that exist can sometimes become a matter of life and death. The substandard and overcrowded nature of housing in major cities means we are seeing more and more tragic events such as fires engulfing buildings. Whether it is cladding that should never have been put on a building in the first place, or the building regulations themselves not being up to scratch, or poor supervision by local authorities of the relevant standards, or perhaps the evermore creative ways found by developers aiming to squeeze every pound out of a project – these all contribute to a climate in which more and more lives are put at risk. When a home is overcrowded, and the building has a poor structural and safety record, fires ignite in the most innocuous ways and end up killing children in their sleep. It is undoubtedly the case that in the tragic example of Grenfell Tower in 2017, the situation was made much more dangerous by a combination of overcrowding and misguided instructions to 'stay put' in these buildings. In the years that followed Grenfell, we have come to the realisation that an estimated 500,000 people have been living in housing with unsafe cladding, until recently often bearing the crushing costs of renovations to make their death-trap properties safe and fire marshals to patrol the sites at night. And it is always the poor, the left-behind, those with no choice but to inhabit such unsafe spaces, who are the first victims.

Quite recently – and not before time – we have seen some political will to take action. Michael Gove, the latest Secretary of State to grapple with the housing crisis, has been predominantly occupied by the cladding issue. In January 2022, in an open letter to the housebuilding industry, he challenged the industry to come up with a solution to the issue, and fast. And then came a threat: to use 'all steps necessary' to get them to comply and ensure that the industry does not fail 'to take responsibility'. A later letter in March 2022 spoke about the possibility of the government imposing 'a solution in law' should there be none forthcoming in due course. Only time will tell whether any of this shall lead to meaningful change. But I am left wondering whether the building industry feels any threat at all; a climate of political volatility and the transient nature of our electoral processes means that in due course Mr Gove will either be moved on or out of government. All the industry would have to do is bide its time.

Generational conflict

I spend a lot of my working life at planning public inquiries. Inquiries are held to examine the refusal of planning permission, often for a major housing development. What makes these quasi-judicial, part formal proceedings, part public meetings quite unique in terms of how we consent to developments in our communities is that all members of the local community are invited to attend and share their views. But, as so often, not all contributors are created equal.

Of the 'civilians' who have the time and energy to participate in planning inquiries, and crucially the interest in doing so, the overwhelming majority are those already on the property ladder. These objectors usually have genuine concerns for their communities: they are afraid of how quickly it is changing, sometimes without their acquiescence. They see the planning system as something done *to* them, as opposed to a system of policies and technicalities, which is also designed to be democratic.

They are not necessarily wrong: many things are 'done' to people within a regulated state, it's just that on most occasions we do not positively seek to stop it. They are experiencing an active intervention in their local landscape and environment. Those objecting to proposals are invariably of an older generation, people who bought their own homes decades ago and who have seen the equity within them rise to a point where they would not be able to afford the same home today, and it is, many times over, their most significant and valuable asset. But while some object for sensible and legitimate reasons, it is sadly often the case that they are fiercely resistant to any sort of change. They are concerned about their own property prices, and while not long ago they dared not say so (because it is not regarded as a material consideration), people are now increasingly open about the fact that they do not want to see the major transformation of a place where they have lived and raised families. It is a decision to believe that land, once built on, can be preserved, absolutely free of any further development; or that development can just go elsewhere, so long as it is not here, next to *my* home.

But there is also often another, less frequently voiced assumption: that what is a basic right to some people may not be seen as such by others. Instead, it has become more of an earned right. And this is why you hear so many older generations talk about how it was hard for them, too, when they bought their own homes, that they took risks and made sacrifices, despite the fact that today's challenges to secure housing are incomparable.

It is hard not to see them as selfish; it is hard to not to look at them and see people who do not care about the next generation. All those horrible experiences I had growing up in squalid places come flashing back when I hear their complaints about loss of light, or loss of trees, or the change in traffic. I don't mean to suggest that their points of view are negligible, or to caricature them when each case is, of course, unique to the individual. The points they make are often highly pertinent, if not the showstoppers they are portrayed as. Indeed, sometimes I represent these people's cases myself. But it is hard not to notice just how devoid people who have benefited from the system can sometimes be of empathy, understanding and compassion. They want to see all developers as greedy and unscrupulous money-grabbing entities completely disinterested in benefiting the public. This may be true, but it is also a fact that these houses (with the exception of the off-plan high-end London schemes sold in Hong Kong) will foster new communities. Young people will raise families and build connections and relationships, start businesses, sit on school boards, revitalise the area. Who knows, those people might well, one day, turn up at an inquiry to resist the proposed development next to them – a form of progress in one sense. I remember questioning one vociferous objector in Kent about his reasons for not wanting a particular development to go forward, given that he was a beneficiary of a housing project next door that was barely 25 years old. Without a hint of irony, he continued his protestations.

As a homeowner myself, I can understand the trepidation around seeing all you've known transformed in an instant, but I also think to myself: where is the inter-generational solidarity in all this? Chances are that their own children would not be able to afford the very houses they currently own. Surely they would like to address the yawning gap between their generation and the current one, rather than taking positive steps to widen this gap for the generation that follows? Surely they empathise with those young people who have seen the opportunities available to their parents slip away from them?

Sadly, all too often the opposite is the case, and solidarity stops at the boundary of the individual family unit. Take the example of the so-called 'bank of mum and dad': in 2020, gifts from parents, grandparents, friends and relatives were said to be behind more than half of house purchases among the under-35s. These same parents who can afford to assist their children with such a major purchase will undoubtedly have also been able to ensure they came of age in a stable and consistent environment: a double-whammy financial and emotional inheritance of riches. The people objecting, wealthy enough to help their own children, solve their own specific inter-generational conflict, ensuring that wealth is maintained within the family for another generation. There has been increasing comment on the millennial 'inheritance boom' that will occur when the baby-boomer generation begin to die off, releasing their wealth into the next generation (who will themselves be getting on a bit – the average age of inheritance is projected to be 61). This evidently won't solve the problems that millennials and Gen Z face now, but because the baby-boomer wealth is unequally distributed across society, it is also likely to exacerbate existing inequality, creating a sort of time-bomb effect – over 80 per cent of millennial homeowners have parents who own their own home, whereas among their non-homeowning peers, the figure is more like 50 per cent. It might seem dramatic to see the future breakdown of society in a local planning inquiry, but to me it often seems inescapable.

So, who represents the voice of the very people who might one day benefit from these homes being built? Well, they don't have time to spare to turn up at a planning inquiry taking place in the local town hall on a Tuesday morning. They are probably working too hard to save up for a deposit, for a home that may not be built, and their voices are therefore absent in a forum that's making crucial decisions about their future. It is of incredibly low priority for someone who is not opposed to or aggrieved by a development to put their head above the parapet, to go out of their way, be motivated enough to voice support for a development, and actually give a better representation of what would benefit the community.

A convenient scapegoat

In all of this, there's one convenient scapegoat. You will often hear governments of all stripes explain that they will offer 'reform', which will transform the planning system. They promise a simplification of the process, which will take us out of this ongoing crisis. If only we came up with some quick ideas, policies and a dash of ingenuity, we would only need about 20 minutes to put the whole mess straight, is the implication. These attempts at reform usually begin with blame being put on the planning system, and in particular how it seeks to 'stifle progress'.

It would be remiss not to admit at this point that the English planning system is perhaps one of the most complicated, convoluted and layered codes anywhere in the world. Its aims and remit are broad – from culture (protection of historic buildings) to ecology (natural environment standards, which are supposed to fulfil national and international obligations), to health and safety. They are supposed to help us deliver a sufficient supply of homes, reignite a strong, competitive economy, promote sustainable transport and result in attractive, pleasant places where people actually want to live, while still ensuring that we meet the challenges of things like climate change, flooding and coastal erosion. Like some of the buildings it condemns, the planning system carries more weight than it can frankly bear.

However, I managed to contain my excitement when, in August 2020, the British government released their ideas for reforming the planning system as a whole. The government led by Boris Johnson was yet to complete its first year in office and, presumably feeling as though the momentum remained with them, they clearly thought that this was the time to be bold. It was trailed as unprecedented change, 'radical reform unlike anything we have seen since the Second World War'. A 'whole new planning system for England' was promised. A 'bonfire of red tape'.

And, following a consultation, and some vociferous feedback, the white paper has not been seen again, presumed dead. Its chief proponent, Dominic Cummings, has since disappeared into the night, the minister for housing and planning policy has changed, and we now have a government in complete disarray at a time of great uncertainty. Between 2019 and 2020, 210,690 properties have been built, of which 168,920 were private enterprise and 3,370 were local authority.

Boris Johnson was right about one thing when he described the planning system as 'designed and built in 1947, it has, like any building of that age, been patched up here and there over the decades'. Over the decades it has been in place, it has undoubtedly become more complex, with the introduction of politically expedient changes, overlaid with national, local and sometimes international requirements, which ostensibly are meant to make our lives better. But all too often this has made the system too complicated for the general public it is meant to serve. Complexity, of course, means loopholes and opportunities for argument, leading to delay, additional cost, resorting to the legal process, and ultimately transforming the whole system unnecessarily into a legalistic one.

If the planning system is in crisis, then, it has a lot to do with changes that have occurred at local government level in the previous decades. The planning system in simple terms is a process of conscious interventions through legislation, policy and decisions, which then affect future development. This is often led by promises made by politicians, local and national, with the main overall aim being to develop places with a view (in practice, their view) to achieving the social, environmental and economic objectives of a country. These include promises to build more homes within a parliament, to do more about climate change through the planning system, or to increase affordable housing, which is almost entirely led by the private sector (although this ought not to be confused with social housing). As I've noted, this often translates to a patchwork of different obligations and aims built up, mostly unmet, by successive governments.

It's also hard to tell who is in charge: local authorities have significant amounts of power to control, give consent, enforce contraventions and ultimately shape how this is put into practice. But at the same time they lack the resources, expertise and finances to be able to do this proactively and effectively. In particular, they have much less power than they once did to build homes. Since 2010 central government funding cuts have reached nearly 50 per cent, as a result of the austerity measures introduced by the Coalition government. The cuts also masked some gerrymandering, which led to the austerity measures falling disproportionately on urban (mainly Labour) authorities. Which means that local authorities continue to provide their statutory functions, the consequence of which leads to the diversion of resources away from non-legally protected areas, in this instance the planning and enforcement departments. It is for this reason that for many local authorities the guillotine fell on the planning departments, with senior staff retiring early (and the institutional knowledge departing with them), and the poor retention of new recruits, who were often expected to do multiple people's jobs at significantly less pay than they would get in the private sector. The substantial fees paid by developers are not channelled back into the planning departments; instead the sums go into the general local authority pot – invariably to be spent elsewhere. Inertia, incompetence, political interference, lack of morale and leadership, delay, a sense of a 'siege mentality' against developers and disgruntled local opposition groups, and many other factors, mean that planning departments across the country are at best ineffective, and at worst actively stifling progress.

Part of that fundamental transformation over multiple decades is the collapse in council housing being built by local authorities. We are then left to the private sector to meet the ever-rising demand – housebuilders who wish to build homes at a rate that they can sell, at a market price that they can sustain. This makes complete sense from a market forces perspective, but it is to the great detriment of the rest of society, because it means that the pace and character of the building is predominantly, if not exclusively, driven by the need to make a healthy profit. This is also exacerbated by the planning requirements placed upon new developments, which require these developments to cross-subsidise a whole number of other planning obligations such as schools, GP practices, open spaces and road improvements, to name a few. This is because local and national policies require that all new developments contribute the necessary infrastructure to make it sustainable and acceptable. This isn't a bad idea in principle, but it will affect any company's bottom line, and the saving needs to come from somewhere – usually selling houses at a particular price point.

So, is there a problem with the planning system in principle?

In simple terms, absolutely there is. But the sorry state of affairs present in the modern planning system is not some abstract issue that can be fixed by a switch, or a 'bonfire of red tape'. It is not some kind of 'blob' acting independently from the rest of us. The planning structures are a product of our political system responding ineffectively to our social needs, over multiple decades; it is what politicians and decision-makers think we need, where and how they believe we wish to live, pushed through the sieve of a highly technical and detailed system combined with ever-changing political priorities. It is a system that many governments have sought unsuccessfully to grapple with, only to either give up mid-way, creating more mess en route, or to tinker with without thought for the long term. The reality is that the system is a reflection of all of us, or perhaps it really reflects a poor understanding of what we want at the expense of what we desperately need; it represents our hopes and ambitions as articulated in convoluted legislation and complex policy, applied by decision makers in a way that ultimately stunts our growth.

This is all intertwined with the legislative

frameworks, the kind of parliament that legislates for it, and the quality and effectiveness of that legislation. Three examples come to mind. In 1990 and 2004, two pieces of legislation were enacted: the Town and Country Planning Act and later, the Planning and Compulsory Purchase Act. Both came forth at a time of stronger political majorities and much greater political consensus about what was needed, and they were legislated for to a pretty clear standard, albeit leaving gaps for policy to fill in. But from 2010 onwards, our governments have tended to be much weaker and/or riven with internal divisions, which are then reflected in poor wording, rushed legislation and compromises between factions and competing ideologies. A classic example is the Localism Act of 2011, which I will discuss further below. It is also true that the decreasing quality of MPs, their lack of engagement with complex issues and technical details, has played a role – something which worsened from 2015 onwards, only to become seriously acute post 2019. There are also some clear conflicts of interest: under

David Cameron's leadership, for example, 39 per cent of Conservative MPs were landlords. The national average is 2 per cent.

The planning system is created ostensibly for the benefit of people who are in reality completely unable to understand how it works. It is a culmination of long and exclusionary technical discussions about planning for cities, towns, parishes and villages. Discussions which in theory the public have access to, but which in practice – in the way they are conducted, the language in which they are communicated, when and where they take place – exclude the majority of them. The process is too often dominated by those who have huge financial interests in the outcome: the major house-builders, the pension funds with long-standing land interests and the well-off minority who do not want development to happen at all are just a few examples. Our housing policy is meant to be about growing society for the majority, and also boosting the economy for the benefit of the many, but it is in this convoluted system that we now find ourselves caught: not having enough homes, not having enough quality homes and generally failing to provide for our future, in the shadow of a pandemic that only deepened our disparities.

In this sense, the planning system has failed in its most basic function – to plan properly for our future. This is what people should have in mind when they think the planning system does not work. Not the picture of some 'unaccountable' bureaucrat sitting in a council office, or the unelected 'man from Bristol', as planning inspectors are pejoratively termed (the Planning Inspectorate HQ being based in Bristol).

The Localism Act of 2011 was sold as a pioneering piece of legislation seeking to find more ways to devolve powers away from Westminster, so that local people could be given more control over how their community developed. Out of it came Neighbourhood Plans, a mechanism to allow local involvement in the development process through which communities decided for themselves how much development they would like to have,

and where. More devolution over these kinds
of important decisions can only be a good
thing; but what came out of the Neighbourhood Plans that were adopted has, in truth,
had mixed results. From my own experience,
it has encouraged many well-meaning people
who care about their communities to use the
process to stifle progress and the number of
houses built. Alternatively, their decisions have
not always been as representative of what the
majority of the local community would like
to see in order to provide for the next generation. It has meant Local Plans, which are
ostensibly prepared and written by borough
and district councils, but with the hands of
communities holding the pen. Anecdotally, it
sounds like neither young people nor those
most affected have been involved in the process
enough. This may be partly down to their lack
of time, an inability to navigate a convoluted
and complicated system, or perhaps a feeling
of intimidation or hopelessness – that their
voices in the matter, which will impact their
daily lives in years down the line, rather than in

the present moment of struggle, will inevitably be disregarded anyway.

Owning a home

The Elizabethan barrister, jurist and later chief justice Sir Edward Coke is often cited in a case about whether sheriffs had the right to enter one's home in the seventeenth century, declaring that 'the house of every one is to him as his Castle and Fortress, as well for his defence against injury and violence, as for his repose'. Which in today's language is often abbreviated to 'an Englishman's home is his castle'.

In 2015, I became a homeowner, moving into a four-bedroomed house in Wembley, with a garden. For the first time in my entire life, I had a space I could truly call my own, even if it was predominantly owned by the bank. Nevertheless, I had a place that was mine on paper, to do with it as I wished. There was a genuine shift in my emotional state: no more measuring time and the stability of my residence according to the next tenancy agreement cycle; no more thinking about what to do when the

estate agents tell me it will cost £100 for them
to reprint the same agreement with only the
date changed; no more thinking about how
to convince a landlord to spend money they
do not want to spend, on a problem that they
care little about. This shift, though, came with
its own responsibilities. It came with a different type of burden, even if it was one that I
was prepared to happily bear. It came with
unprecedented financial responsibility, and in
some ways it was the first time I appreciated
what adulthood actually meant. It meant being
completely present in my own surroundings,
and slightly daunted that I was responsible for
every nook and cranny, but also excited at the
fact that the option of calling the landlord to
fix something no longer existed. To think back
to the semi-slum of Nairobi where my family
had one bedroom, and one living room opposite the toilet and kitchen. We were among the
most privileged of our neighbours, sharing
this space only as six or seven people at a time.
At least it had clean running water and sanita-
tion, but it was not the kind of environment

one might choose willingly; the lack of paving turned the streets into flowing mud at a little drop of rain. To think back to even more crowded rooms, this time in Britain, far from the slums but a different kind of squalor at the heart of a major global capital city. I had been on the move for so many years, most of the time not by choice. Small bursts of stability in university accommodation, house shares and mini couch-surfing and flat-sitting episodes had all been building up to the security I now enjoy.

To then have come back to where it all began for me, right here in Wembley, where I am now a member of my local residents' association, and the chair of the Safer Neighbourhood Ward Panel, feels profound. A place where I find myself helping to write and distribute the quarterly newsletter informing my neighbours of updates, where I take my son to the volunteer-run community walled garden. The precise moment when I settled my roots here can be traced back now: the historical records kept in the Land Registry shall bear my name and that of my father and his father before him.

This new feeling of rootedness brought with it a real sense of pride: I felt a subtle difference in my stature every morning as I closed the door behind me. This type of feeling has an impact on your life: it affects how you see yourself as someone who has a stake in this community. After living in Wembley for so long, it made me feel like someone who has a future to build within this place, a place to generate a lifetime of memories. It has a role to play in my desire to find a community, to invest in that community, to build friendships in those surroundings. To find and hold on to that which you will one day pass on to the next generation.

Now not everyone may see home ownership in the same way, still less seek it, but for those who do this feeling is a privilege that is currently denied to too many people, even more so against the backdrop of a situation in which other forms of long-term, financially viable homemaking, like council tenancies, have disappeared. I believe it lies at the bottom of the fragmented, unhappy society we see emerging before our eyes; not just in the conflict between the generations, but more generally between the haves and have nots, those the status quo serves and those it doesn't.

Of course, some people like the freedom of a short-term let, or the lack of hassle that comes with never being responsible for your own boiler. Some feel drawn to the possibilities of co-operative ownership, or see the private rental protections in cities like Berlin as the way forward. But the desire to own does have a particular place in the psyche of the British people: Sir Edward Coke's case enshrined an idea of the home as autonomous sanctuary, where arbitrary external decisions could not trespass into private space. In Britain we rarely have a meaningful discussion around what it means to have this kind of security without necessarily owning the bricks and mortar that protect it. We just assume that owning is now and will remain always the gold standard. Politically, we never seem to contemplate a scenario where that may not always be necessary; instead, we obsess about the housing ladder: whether people can get on it, how people can get help to climb it, why not enough people have a chance to try. Governments resort to promoting mortgages that require only a 5 per cent deposit as a way of building a 'property owning' democracy, perhaps because they too see owning a home as providing a stake in society, laying the groundwork for an electorate invested in their shared vision. The Right to Buy scheme championed by Margaret Thatcher's government was always described as building a generation of new homeowning Conservative voters. More recently, the Help to Buy schemes and the stamp duty holidays are also examples of policy levers designed to extend the chances of more people owning their own homes. But notwithstanding the short-term freeze on evictions during Covid-19, how many examples of improving security of tenure for renters can we think of? Or measures to ensure that building standards are properly maintained, or that more landlords are being held to account for the substandard properties they put onto the market.

Too often, the housing market feels like

some giant Ponzi scheme in which we are all being forced to take part, and if we are not part of it we face the consequences of a world of insecure lets and being at the mercy of unscrupulous landlords or languishing on decades-long council waiting lists. Only a couple of years ago the government finally clamped down on the extortionate fees levied on tenants by estate agents charging for 'administration', references and renewing contracts. Some of these high fees, when added to the need to provide one month's rent in advance and the same sum as a deposit, all at the same time, prove financially debilitating before you've even moved in, or even prevent you from doing so. I remember moving into a house share when all five of us were charged £95 (a significant sum for us at the time) *each* for administration fees when we all signed identical documents, all at the same time.

Unfortunately, instead of more legal recourse to fight these sorts of unrelenting and ruthless practices, we have seen the simplistic, short-term ideas that lead to the demand for housing to go up exponentially without tackling in any meaningful way the supply. There's no attempt to address the poor labour markets and underfunding of public sector jobs. This underfunding means that nurses, junior doctors, recent graduates – people who we were so very recently calling 'key workers' – can often simply not afford to live in major cities. They will have to live elsewhere, hopefully within reasonable commute time, in order to be able to even dream of buying a property.

It is perhaps not surprising that, in a society that collectively and individually obsesses over home ownership as the ultimate goal, once we have scrambled onto the bottom rung of the housing ladder, we suddenly have a direct interest in maintaining the unsustainable and bleak status quo. We become fixated on how much the property has gone up in value since last week, worrying about the impact of that new development just over the road. We engage in this cognitive dissonance of knowing and appreciating how fundamentally unfair the system is, having experienced it first hand, while being glad and relieved to be on the other side of the divide now, holding all the cards, and hoping and praying that it does not all come crashing down on us. Interest rates being kept artificially low represents a prime example of the need to be extremely careful about making adjustments to a highly unstable pyramid that's wobbly and has far too many people clinging onto it for dear life. This, once again, always serves the status quo.

Too much and the wrong kind

It's not true, of course, that no housing is built in Britain. But how much of what is built is what is needed? Private market housebuilders have obligations to build and sell a proportion of 'affordable housing' at a discount to the market price as part of a planning agreement (the same agreement would also provide for a school or other public services). But in reality, as I mentioned earlier, this 'affordable' definition might only be discounted at around 20–30 per cent of the market value, and in many cases it is completely unaffordable to people living locally. And where social housing *has* been provided as part of a mixed-tenure development, the residents of those properties were often segregated, something that later became known as 'poor doors' – where the entrances for social housing residents were separate to those living in the private market part of the same development. In 2019, there were reports of a development in South London in which the children of residents of social accommodation were blocked from using the same playpark as the private renters, instead being provided with a rather bleak-looking 'small strip of toddler play equipment'. This is symptomatic of a wider malaise, too, as is shown by a survey to mark the 100 years since the advent of social housing, which revealed that a quarter of people would 'feel uncomfortable' living close to council and housing association properties. This is an incredibly sad state of affairs to have engulfed what should be one of our proudest achievements as a society.

Meanwhile, from Vancouver to London, major new developments are sold off-plan to

foreign investors with no prospect of local
people, who might actually live in the homes
they purchase, ever having a chance to
compete. In recent months, it has become
abundantly clear that we need to address the
significant and distorting influence of major
global capital on the housing market. It is
simply unsustainable, as well as in many cases
plainly unethical and unfair. It's the way that the
Canadian teacher's pension fund, or the Hong
Kong-based private equity fund, can invest in
prime real estate in London, distorting general
affordability on the way. Russian oligarchs and
Arab sheikhs attempting to shield their wealth
in major capitals and investments are not solely
responsible for the housing shortage crisis, but
I would suggest they play a not insignificant
role. Even if money is being spent at the top of
the market, it creates a ripple effect, driving out
many wealthy Britons, for example, who might
have been able to live close to the centre of
major cities (particularly in London) to instead
settle in boroughs and suburbs further out.
Those who could have traditionally afforded

to get on the housing ladder in the outskirts of cities and towns can no longer afford to buy, or even rent, where their parents may have been able to less than two decades ago. This leads to the kind of gentrification we have seen in so many places; a classic example is Brent, where I continue to live, where places that were once so run down that no one would have seen themselves raising a family there (Queen's Park, Kilburn, Willesden, Harlesden) are all, rather dizzyingly for someone who grew up there, now prime real estate with million-pound houses being quite common.

To me, it shows how the housing market lies at the heart of many of the problems we face today. It is clear that the London property market has for years operated as a laundromat for the money of Russian oligarchs, among others. Somewhat ironically, by gratefully accepting their billions, we seem to have offered them a 'stake in society', or at least in our political system, which puts us in the embarrassing position of having undermined our own attempts to take action against them after the invasion of Ukraine in February 2022. 'The fear is that Russian money is so entrenched in London now that the opportunity to use it as leverage against Putin could be lost,' a source in Washington said. 'Putin doesn't hold his money abroad, it is all in the kleptocrats' names and a hell of a lot of it is sitting in houses in Knightsbridge and Belgravia right under your government's noses.'

Even before the invasion finally prompted some sluggish movement on this issue, the BBC's *Panorama* programme had revealed leaked documents detailing the wealth and dealings of world leaders, politicians and billionaires. Notable perhaps was the significant land and property holdings of the very rich and powerful: the King of Jordan has secretly amassed UK and US property worth £70 million.

The million-pound mega-mansion in Belgravia or other parts of Central London might seem a world away from the struggle of a young couple trying to buy their first home in a Cornish holiday town, or a teenager trying to revise for his A levels while sharing his bedroom with two younger siblings. And in some ways it is. But if we ignore the deep connections that lie between all these things, we are ignoring the importance of housing and how it can be seen so differently depending on the constituency and their particular interest – as a market, as a resource, as a human right, as a pension pot, as an investment or a way of protecting interests. The scandal of Londongrad, exposed by the Pandora Papers and the war in Ukraine, is in some ways just the logical conclusion of treating the housing market as something other than a home; as a place to store cash as opposed to live life. While this of course is a smaller part of a much bigger domestic and existing inequity, to ignore it would be not to fully appreciate the bigger picture. It is unfair, and it cannot be right for successive governments to facilitate the conditions that lead to the people who elected them to be so drastically disadvantaged by those same conditions, only for the governments to be forced into situations that require them to either subsidise the living of their citizens through welfare spending, or indeed just kick the can down the road without ever confronting reality.

Where next?

Beginning with 1979, we let the genie out of the bottle. The Labour Party, academics and some in the Conservative Party warned against the foreseeable consequence of selling off so much social housing. It is therefore not entirely accurate to say that this is all now with the benefit of hindsight. This is most certainly not to say that Britain was the land of milk and honey before 1979; the decade that preceded it saw Britain go through a hugely tumultuous time, with governments falling frequently and an unprecedented intervention into Britain's economy by the International Monetary Fund, all culminating in the Winter of Discontent. But it was following the liberalisation of the economy, after 1979, that we really began to fail to grapple with planning properly for the future. We undermined the crucial role of local authorities as a body responsible for managing local change with adequate resources, we were mistaken to believe that more local involvement would mean contentment in the process, and we ultimately put too much faith in a skewed market dominated by a few self-interested housebuilders. We failed to properly appreciate that we live in a labour market whose participants will never earn enough to live to the standards of the generation before them. And by the time we got to 1997, it was a done deal, which would be difficult to reverse; a Labour Party that transformed investment in the NHS and reduced child poverty still didn't do enough to tackle the housing crisis. If you tune in to panel shows like *Any Questions?* or *Newsnight*, you'll still hear politicians on all sides blaming each other and throwing statistics back and forth – something that is, of course, a lot easier and perhaps more satisfying than attempting to actually do something about it. But if we do not take these major steps now, when will we? It was only in March 2022 that the Secretary of State now seeking to grapple with the housing issue, Michael

Gove, said, 'We've essentially got a cartel of volume housebuilders who operate in a particular way and there are all sorts of unhappy consequences.' This is quite punchy stuff from a cabinet minister, and the house-building industry expressed anger at these disparaging comments, highlighting the importance of the industry for jobs and economic activity.

If we are going to make a difference, the truth is that the time for tweaks is over – change needs to be both systemic and radical; change on the level of that which followed the Second World War. The precise mechanism for doing so would be both legislative and procedural, but before all of that it would have to be underpinned by political will and some brave decisions. Fundamentally, the nature of our housing market is that we are too reliant on the private sector, and crucially on a handful of housebuilders who, naturally, have an interest in not oversupplying the market to suit their interests. What we need is local authorities who are not necessarily in competition with the private sector, but rather play a direct role in ensuring that we do not rely on one source only to replace our depleted social housing stock. In any event, any local authority providing more land and resources to building more homes will have to work closely – at least in the short term – with the major housebuilders and anyone else who wishes to be involved in this endeavour.

This need not be imagined from scratch; the Irish example of the Affordable Housing Act 2021, signed into law on 21 July 2021, specifically allows for an expansion of the role of the state in the provision of affordable housing. There is no reason this could not be mirrored here. We have seen the Mayor of London seeking to develop land that is owned by Transport for London with a view to building more social housing. There are new, creative and potentially transformative ideas to help us plug gaps, including the 'modular homes' pioneered by Dutch/British company Modomo – high-quality housing, which is designed to be erected on unused urban sites, before being dismantled and moved elsewhere when the site is earmarked for permanent development

– which assists in the short to medium term. Coliving, although not the cheapest option out there, has emerged as a modern form of shared housing that is attractive to many young professional people. It gives them access to a shared community, an opportunity to connect with people from all walks of life, in a safe and often high-quality environment where they can build new experiences.

This is all to be welcomed, but for the moment these remain timid steps seeking to address a colossal problem. The government speaks about building 300,000 homes by the mid 2020s (these figures include conversions of houses into flats as well as just new builds); I firmly believe that this is not only a grossly inadequate target, but one that plainly will not be achieved if the current climate does not change drastically. Not least given that we have failed to meet this target for some time.

Let's consider the gradual stripping of powers from local authorities, weakening their ability to effect local change. The centralisation of power, the delegation of some local control to Neighbourhood Plans and the lack of resources means that local government is just ineffective. I believe that we not only need to give an enormous amount of resources to local authorities and their planning departments, we also need the infrastructure to support this major shift in order to manage it effectively and efficiently. We need politicians who are embedded in their local communities, who play a significant role in setting out a vision that truly represents a sustainable future. Who are brave enough to make tough local decisions for the majority's benefit, irrespective of the electoral consequences, with a view to thinking strategically and for the long-term betterment of their communities. Some might say that this is naïve given how the short-term electoral cycle determines so much these days, but to be frank our democratic processes today are part of the problem rather than part of the solution. We need more decisions based on what is best for the common good rather than what is palatable to an overactive minority of voters. Once that strategic direction has been set, politicians just need to get out of the way, becoming high-level managerial CEOs who need only intervene when the direction of travel looks troubled, when the quality of homes is being diluted, when standards need to be monitored closely and people need to be held accountable. What they cannot do is allow the minority on whose votes they rely to hijack the process to the detriment of the majority.

This is hard stuff, particularly when it means inviting politicians to make decisions that may mean that they lose political power: these are the same radical ideas, which could transform our society for the better, that have frightened people, and by extension the politicians who rely on their votes. We see far too many short-sighted councillors, driven largely by their fear of vocal constituents resistant to change. Many of these stand for election on platforms that either seek to block the adoption of a Local Plan, or to cynically abandon or stifle the very Local Plan they have themselves adopted (which specifically requires them to make land available for housing) if it looks like it will cost them votes. And it seems that voters are very much willing to punish MPs who step out of line: the Chesham and Amersham by-election in June 2021, in which the sitting Conservative MP was ousted by a Liberal Democrat, took place soon after the consultation period for the Planning for the Future white paper had concluded, and was widely assumed to represent voters rebelling against planning reforms and the HS2 rail link. These are real-time responses at the ballot box to any proposals for radical change. The reality is that there are formidable vested interests on many sides, which require facing down by a government that is prepared to lose votes, and not win many friends, for the greater good. Meanwhile the same local authorities being run by coalitions opposed to any change are simultaneously missing the professional support and expertise, lacking in any strategic direction, and besieged by planning appeals overturning their unreasonable decisions, sometimes costing hundreds of thousands of pounds a year in legal costs.

All the while, with every year that passes, not enough homes are being built and the insatiable demand continues unabated. Essentially, every meaningful progress made in the short term is rendered meaningless by the short passage of time and political change.

In economic commentator Liam Halligan's book on the UK's chronic housing crisis, *Home Truths*, he quotes from a *Times* editorial from 1969:

> It is essential to have not only more houses, but more houses of the required type in the right place. There are technical difficulties that have to be overcome over land, financing and the organisation of the building industry. But there is also the question of will. Housing has not yet achieved the place of priority in official policy justified both by the social suffering involved and the public concern that has been aroused.

Tackling the housing crisis as it is currently constituted is a bit like facing up to the climate crisis. We all know it's a major problem that has now reached an acute point, demonstrated time and again in increasingly desperate and obvious ways. We all know it's strangling our children's future, even while a minority make millions out of it. If only we were bold enough to bite the bullet. If only we were prepared to sustain an effort over two consecutive parliaments, or when people weren't looking. Yes, the climate crisis may be the number-one concern of our time, but the housing crisis is a similar principle, only in microcosm: a decent, clean, stable and safe place to call home for your lifetime is a fundamental human right. Nor are the two crises unrelated: we do not have to look very far to see the impact of floods, erosion and storms, and if sea levels rise at a fraction of the predicted amount, much of the south coast will be severely affected. And nor is the solution impossible to imagine; we know what the answers are already, we just need to implement them. The ideas I suggest in the following pages can make a significant difference to the lives of many millions. They're imperfect and I do not profess to suggest they are either completely new, or will completely resolve the current predicament – but they would at least be a start, and if they do not seem entirely original it merely underlines the extent to which we already know the answers to this crisis. We just need to act, now and with resolution.

First, we need better leadership at all levels, and this also requires a more energised electorate, a better-informed citizenry demanding that their needs are met effectively. At the moment, we have endless interfering, and very little *accountability* and *sustainability*. We certainly cannot solve the housing crisis, just as we cannot resolve the climate crisis, unless there is the political impetus, will and determination to confront the problem, including taking difficult, unpopular decisions. This means that when reform is proposed, the legislation underpinning it is drafted, and decisions taken to implement this, it is with the clear aim of ensuring lives and livelihoods are improved for the *majority*. Not whether these steps are going to impact the next local and national elections.

Not whether the decisions are going to be politically palatable, and certainly not ensuring that those for whom the status quo currently works are not negatively affected. And while there is no guarantee that every grateful home-owner will bless its name should they succeed, what I am suggesting first and foremost will be about avoiding greater unpopularity later – a growing legacy of commitment to society on behalf of those who are losing out, especially young people. Some stability in the leadership, too, is essential; that we have had 20 housing ministers since 1997, and more pertinently 12 since 2010, with the average posting lasting just 1.25 years, is a scandal. How are we going to tackle such a serious problem with this lack of consistency, this lack of dedication, and certainly no real political will?

Again, I am not naïve enough to think that this is going to be easy. I am not blind enough to ignore that fresh legislation and significant collaboration and coordination is required. I am fully conscious of the fact that the easy thing to do is to simply oppose all development that comes forward. When you think about how much of a political hot potato, for example, building in the green belt is, it is no wonder that politicians are much more likely to be short-sighted – this is the easy way out. When decisions made in a council can have a direct electoral response at a ward level, politicians are obviously unlikely to behave like turkeys being asked to vote for Christmas. Which means there is also an obligation on us, the electorate – and especially those of us who have the security, time and resources to engage with local government, attend meetings, write letters and so on – to think not just about ourselves, but about what is good for our society as a whole. Those with the greatest amount to lose (although most of the time this will be a perceived rather than a real loss) must come to accept change, and not view it with suspicion. This is why I am myself supporting various initiatives to better inform the general public, elected councillors, charities, campaign groups and the media, giving them a more simplified and nuanced view of our processes.

Could it become a reality: a world where someone could see their home as their greatest and perhaps only asset in life, and still be interested in the possibility that more homes be introduced into their locality and not see this as a threat? I cannot be certain, but the longer the state continues to believe that it can all be 'left to the market', the more the crisis shall deepen, the more people without the resources and wherewithal to compete will be left behind, and the more we continue to build an economy and society working predominantly for a small minority, while a growing majority has no real prospect of catching up. In the meantime, we simply waste the energy and potential of literally millions of people caught in the insecure housing trap, as well as children growing up in exactly the kind of stultifying, deadening environment my siblings and I did.

In this respect, perhaps, does the fundamental problem with our processes (decision making, the planning system as a whole, plan making, etc.) illustrate a larger malaise with our democracy? Can it really be possible to have liberal, free-market economies where it will be simultaneously possible to meet the demands and hopes of *all* citizens, *without* significant and wide-ranging state interventions in the housing market? Is it possible to make plans for the future, with a view to allocating vast amounts of land for development, when those living in those communities, who also happen to be more likely to vote, will consider this a threat to what they have always known? The pandemic has shown that the government is willing to intervene in an unprecedented manner when it matters, so why not now?

Second, councils need both the legal powers and the practical resources to build social housing. This is not about imagining a utopia; it is quite literally in living memory. This will inevitably still require working closely with the private sector housebuilders, and it will not be cheap: land prices, construction costs, infrastructure, resourcing and materials, employing those who have the requisite skills, upskilling those who do not, are some examples of what is needed to meet the challenge.

We know that from the early 1980s the powers enjoyed by local authorities to do something meaningful about housing have been stripped away. They have been unable to raise the funds they need (although the lifting of the cap on a council's ability to borrow against the value of their housing stock was a welcome recent step change) or recruit and retain essential expertise, and the selling off of their housing stock has further diminished the contributions they can make to those most in need. This also means that we stop relying on a few large-scale housebuilders who have been the direct beneficiaries of the status quo, themselves relying on local authorities to make decisions despite having lost the expertise required to assess highly complicated planning applications. While most developers would also tell you that they wish to get on and build, it is often the case that moving slower suits their interests, by controlling supply rather than flooding the market.

The National Housing Federation, which represents housing associations, has similarly talked about building quicker, and the role that new technologies and techniques could play – such as construction methods that would allow homes to be built in factories and subsequently built on site more quickly and to high standards. Modomo, whose work I mentioned earlier, is developing projects for spaces in cities currently not being used to their full potential, perhaps utilised for car parking or open storage. It might be land in a phase of a longer-term regeneration project that will take 10, 15, 20 years to bear fruit. The initial upfront design work is really important, and the standard of the build is of the highest quality. For all intents and purposes you would not notice the difference between this or any other new build. They seek to provide living space for a minimum of seven years, or a maximum of 15 years, depending on the term of the free space they're currently occupying. This is a product that's seeking to address the housing crisis now. With planning permission resolved, these apartments could be built and in situ in less than a year. These are the sorts of flexible, exciting and innovative ideas that we need to embrace in the short term while we grapple with the more long-term structural issues. Together with a healthier, more competitive relationship between private developers, this would go some way to relieving the pressures of supply we face in the housing market today.

Third, while the usual points around supply and demand, as well as the problems around the planning system, are well rehearsed, reforming the banking and mortgage market is also a crucial component of the wider picture. The Tony Blair Institute for Global Change published some fascinating research explaining that addressing the issue of supply is only likely to have a modest impact on house prices over a generation. We need to also address mortgage finance; particularly around making the mortgage market more accessible to buyers who cannot afford the large deposits, or fall back on the bank of mum and dad. This would be in order to help so many responsible renters paying other people's mortgages for decades without ever getting a chance to do the same for themselves, and become responsible first-time borrowers. This would be wholly separate to the Help to Buy schemes discussed earlier, which only stoke up the demand and too often assist those least in need of help to get on the property ladder. Instead, these proposed reforms would be about the *redistribution* of credit towards first-time buyers most in need, rather than increasing the volume of lending in a way that may ultimately destabilise the market as a whole.

The scarcity of land on this island is also a major consideration, but it is more accurately a question of scarcity of land where people find it easier to build. It is about the scarcity of land where people actually wish to live, almost always correlated with where the well-paying jobs are so that they can afford to buy. There is then the spatial aspect of this: there is plenty of land on this island, it's just that there are many places where people do not want to live. This must also change if we are to be bold, to build new settlements, connected and inter-connected. New centres that imagine new communities planting new roots. Where there will be good jobs, schools, hospitals and opportunities for those who are brave enough to go and live there.

CONCLUSIONS

Immense though the challenge of the housing crisis is, perhaps we have reached a tipping point. We are now in danger of losing an entire generation to the housing precariousness that I grew up with. We are in danger of learning nothing from the mistakes we have made in the past, of becoming overwhelmed and paralysed by the scale of the challenge in the same way we are by climate change. We are, frankly, in danger of undermining our national security (and that of other countries) through sheer greed, in the process creating a societal instability the likes of which we have never seen, in our own country and elsewhere, as well as the ethically damaging effect of tolerating such sheer inequality generally.

This is not a crisis that blew up overnight, but rather one years in the making. Years of compounded mistakes, and lack of political will to do something about it. It began with a decade in which well-earned and ambitiously executed plans to reimagine a nation in a fraught post-war period, in order to meet the demands of its citizens after a horrific chapter in our history, began to run in reverse. Through the 1980s and 1990s homes slowly evolved from people's safe sanctuaries, a place of dignity and safety, to becoming seen as commodities and a haven for people's financial investments; the dissipating of social housing for political expediency and short-sighted decisions on behalf of those in charge followed in lockstep. It is certainly arguable that the scale of the challenge we face today is comparable to what was confronted in those years post 1918 and 1945. In 2019, 17 per cent of housing (and 25 per cent of privately rented housing) was rated non-decent, defined as representing 'a hazard of immediate threat to a person's health, not in reasonable state of repair, lacking modern facilities or not effectively insulated or heated'. This time we are not attempting to recover from devastation caused by war, but rather many years of neglect, failure to act and much more, as well as a global pandemic and a dramatic crash in living standards. But what we are missing now, compared to the inter-war period, is the political consensus to do something about it, to offer some kind of vision for the future.

What we have at the moment is not a system fit for purpose. It is highly technical, overly legalistic, and driven largely by the minority who have the time, the interests and frankly the wherewithal to engage in it. The rest of society is excluded as the forum is vacated in favour of the experts who all too often understand the details in a technical matter but are too far removed from the daily lives of the ordinary people. It is a desperately sad state of affairs when, conceptually, most of us see our homes as that safe haven to live, grow up, make memories and build a life in, while for many others it is more akin to a financial investment, a pension pot, an inheritance, which speaks to the life lived, similar to gold, stocks and shares. The gulf between these two realities, I believe, speaks to the deep and persisting inequalities of modern life. This mismatch is the pressing concern of our time. And unfortunately it is only getting worse.

It is undoubtedly a housing crisis, a crisis of legislation and policy, of bricks and mortar and planning permission. It is a crisis deeply and ironically embedded in our cultural references, of what it means to be as 'safe as houses', safe for a few, and unsafe for so many others. But it is also an economic, social and moral crisis, a challenge to our current understanding of how economic and labour markets are structured, and of where the moral centre of our society lies. That the status quo only works for the few and the lucky, with the many and the unfortunate bearing the brunt of this broken system, is both unsustainable and profoundly unfair. It is not simply a matter of policy and technical details; it is about people's lives, futures, ambitions, and the limits being placed on what they will be able to achieve during their own lifetimes.

As Dr Deborah Potts has pointed out in my radio documentary *Planning, Politics and Housing*, the current labour market in modern capitalist societies is unfit for purpose. This means that people on lower incomes – not least public sector workers doing important work as public servants (think civil servants, police officers, junior doctors and paramedics, nurses and so on) – need help if they are to afford good-quality housing, whether that is to buy or to rent. At the same time, we need to address the exploitative nature of some of the so-called 'gig economy' jobs, which often do not offer much security, career progression or employment rights, often for companies that fail to meaningfully pay back into society in the form of tax. In this wider context it is simply a scandal that – in a country as wealthy as Britain – we are allowing people to live in entirely inadequate housing, in situations where they must choose between paying the rent and having the heating on, and must rely on foodbanks to get by. The idea that healthcare should be freely available (at the point of delivery) to all is deeply ingrained in the British mind, but for some reason human needs that are almost as fundamental – food and shelter – are seen as more optional. Whether or not people are in full-time employment is irrelevant to our obligation to care for them, but it does show the extent to which the game is rigged against even those diligently playing it.

To my mind, this has also led to a crisis in our democratic system. This is why we see governments talk about 'levelling up' society, ensuring that people are not 'left behind' when the very system they continue to support, function within and seek legitimacy from contributes to the dark malaise that is present throughout this country and many democracies and developing nations. However, in a typically cynical and expedient fashion, the current agenda appears to want to pit the North against the South, with the so-called 'red wall' seats purportedly an example of communities in need of 'levelling up'. And while this geographical levelling up seems to be drawn along an arbitrary line in the middle of our isles, the response of some cities, like Sheffield, suggests there may not be an appetite up North to be a convenient and expedient safety valve for the South, and a cynicism about whether whatever investment is forthcoming will also be long-lasting. The Mayor of London has spoken about how much huge parts of London and the South East could do with levelling up too.

Living in a state of constant instability and insecurity, as my family did while I was young, affects your trust in authority and in society at large. Behind the housing crisis, confidence in our society is quietly seeping away. There can be little confidence in a status quo that has no place for the young, the ambitious and those who – reasonably enough – wish to have similar living standards and opportunities to their parents and grandparents. The confidence to believe that you can grow up in relative comfort and safety, in the hope that your children will do a little better than you and much better than those who came before them, is a powerful and important social glue. That promise is no longer guaranteed, and it is made even more bleak when the very place you rest your head on a daily basis cannot be assured. But now more than ever this requires a collective action and resolve of a scale we have never known, for the size of the challenge we face commands us to take steps on a scale we have never known.

To end this book, I want to turn back to Virginia Woolf. She closes her own essay by explaining that 'when I ask you to write more books I am urging you to do what will be for your good and for the good of the world at large'. All of us have a part to play in improving the situation: in who we vote for, how (and how much) we participate in planning inquiries and where our investments are kept. We can also address our abiding prejudices – for example, the persistent maligning of what it means to live in a council home, when in reality it provided overwhelmingly decent, affordable and secure homes. It gave many an opportunity to thrive; it was a luxury that kept us hanging on to the housing waiting list by the tips of our fingers for over a decade. Today, you're somehow meant to feel shame if you don't play your part in dispensing the majority of your income into the pockets of private landlords. We need to address the disparity described here in a meaningful way, to build our communities in a way that ensures the buildings built are not sold off elsewhere, and so that those of a different generation who faced a different marketplace, different housing market and all round different reality come to fully appreciate the immense challenges faced by young people. To confront these points is all for the betterment of our next generation; it is the very reason why we need to do more to unlock so much potential. It is undoubtedly 'for the good of the world at large'.

The musician Morrissey, reflecting on his life on *Desert Island Discs*, mentioned that he 'came from nothing, came from a council house ...' Which tells you really about how we view what it means to have grown up in what is today such a scarce resource. But increasingly, council housing doesn't look like 'nothing' – it looks like the opportunity to live in relative security and stability, in one of the most revolutionary, pioneering and compassionate ways to house people in the post-war period and since. In this sense, Morrissey might have missed the irony of his point: he didn't come from nothing; he enjoyed a privilege that has since all but disappeared.

It has been a long time since I walked past those train tracks on my way to Mahatma Gandhi House. The building itself was sold for £10 million in 2015 by Brent Council, and in the same year a property development company submitted an application to redevelop the site for office space and 198 residential flats. Following referral to the Mayor of London, permission was granted in 2016 – to include only 20 per cent affordable housing, far below Brent's stated target of 50 per cent affordable new homes within the borough.

At the time still called Mahatma Gandhi House, the building was sold again on 25 January 2017 with the benefit of planning permission for £18.2 million, an 85 per cent profit in just two years. None of this is remotely illicit;

it is simply absurd and speaks to the madness of the moment. Millions of pounds of liquid cash profit instantly realised while the rest of us, still walking to whatever new building now hosts the housing department, continue to be stuck in the mud.

Something must be done, and now.

ACKNOWLEDGEMENTS

This book began for me a long time ago, when I was experiencing homelessness and didn't realise it. Now, as a homeowner and as a planning barrister I am able to bring a uniquely timely perspective to it. I am extremely grateful to all those people who have helped me along the way to escape a fate all too real for so many people. This book is above all for them.

I have been extremely lucky to work again with my editor, Cecily Gayford, and as always her fresh perspective and feedback have been invaluable to me during this process. It really has been an honour to collaborate on some of the most intractable issues of our time – as always, ably assisted by the team at Profile Books, including Jon Petre and Valentina Zanca.

Thank you, too, to my copy editor, Hayley Shepherd, and my agent, Jonny Geller.

My gratitude to all the people who took the time to read the book in the early drafts and offer some thoughtful, sometimes brutal, commentary in advance: James Corbet Burcher, Sarah Richards, Simon Ricketts, Peter Goatley QC, Dr Deborah Potts, Samuel Hunt, Lorna Walker, Keith Jenkins, Michael Humphries QC, Kathy Gee, James Stacey, Jonathan Buckwell and Salim Rachid. This book is undoubtedly the better for it. There is always a great deal more I could have explored around this colossal topic, and each complexity could have warranted its own book. Indeed, a number of the problems we see today have a very long tail, and I am only able to focus on some aspects of this. Nevertheless, I do hope to have touched upon the most pressing, salient concerns. As I said in my first book, the purpose of writing is to ignite conversation, dialogue and even disagreement. I want to start a discussion, not conclude one.

There was one person whose feedback I would have undoubtedly gained from immensely, but unfortunately this was not meant to be. Stephen Ashworth, one of two people to whom I have dedicated this book, introduced me to planning law in the first place and he died unexpectedly in May 2021. With a career spanning 30-plus years, he contributed to, and was always extremely passionate about, reshaping communities all over the country. He probably would have said that I am not being radical enough. I will always miss his wise counsel and hope that he would be proud of what I have written here.

No thanks is complete without mentioning my family, who experienced over many years the most appalling living conditions on multiple continents. Fortunately, for most of us this is largely behind us. I thank them for allowing me to share so much of it for the greater aim of bringing to light the lessons for wider society. There are too many, beyond us, who continue to experience similarly poor conditions, or a lack of a fixed abode of any kind – stunting their growth and potential. I hope that this book ignites a sense of urgency.

And of course thanks to my wife, Leila, and our son, Zack. They are the reason I get up every day.

BIBLIOGRAPHY AND SOURCES

Books, Films and Media

Charles Dickens, *Bleak House* (1852–3) (London: Penguin Classics, 2003).

Virginia Woolf, *A Room of One's Own* (London: Hogarth Press, 1929).

Deborah Potts, *Broken Cities: Inside the Global Housing Crisis* (London: Zed Books, 2020).

Josh Ryan-Collins, Toby Lloyd and Laurie MacFarlane, *Rethinking the Economics of Land and Housing* (London: Zed Books, 2017).

Nick Gallent, *Whose Housing Crisis?: Assets and Homes in a Changing Economy* (Bristol: Policy Press, 2019).

Liam Halligan, *Home Truths: The UK's Chronic Housing Shortage* (London: Biteback Publishing, 2019).

Hashi Mohamed, *People Like Us: What it Takes to Make it in Modern Britain* (London: Profile Books, 2020).

Jeremy Sandford, *Cathy Come Home*, dir. Ken Loach, prod. Tony Grant (BBC One, 16 November 1966).

'Morrissey', *Desert Island Discs* (4 December 2009)
<bbc.co.uk/programmes/b00p068y> [accessed 3
May 2022].

Hashi Mohamed, *Planning, Housing and Politics*,
BBC Radio 4 (21 February 2022) <bbc.co.uk/
programmes/m0014ptp> [accessed 3 May 2022].

Anna Minton, *Big Capital: Who Is London For?*
(London: Penguin Random House, 2017).

Jonathan F. P. Rose, *The Well-Tempered City: What
Modern Science, Ancient Civilizations, and Human
Nature Teach Us About the Future of Urban Life* (New
York: HarperCollins, 2016).

Reports, Studies and Government

Bank of England, *Monetary Policy Report: February
2022* (London: February 2022).

Philip Brien, 'Service industries: key economic
indicators', House of Commons Library
<commonslibrary.parliament.uk/research-
briefings/sn02786/#:~:text=The%20service%20
industries%20include%20the,employment%20
in%20April%2DJune%202021> [accessed 26 April
2022].

Adam Corlett and Felicia Odamtten, *Hope to buy:
the decline of youth home ownership*, Resolution
Foundation (December 2021).

Adam Corlett and Lalitha Try, *The Living Standards*

Outlook 2022, Resolution Foundation (London: 2022).

Committee Report: Planning Committee on 9 May 2016, Item No. 4, Case Number 15/4714, Brent Council (9 May 2016).

Joseph Elliott and Rachelle Earwaker, 'Renters on low incomes face a policy black hole: homes for social rent are the answer', Joseph Rowntree Foundation (13 October 2021) <jrf.org.uk/report/renters-low-incomes-face-policy-black-hole-homes-social-rent-are-answer> [accessed 26 April 2022].

Simon Gillespie, *Housing supply: indicators of new supply, England: April to June 2021*, Department for Levelling Up, Housing and Communities (London: 30 September 2021).

Ray Forrest and Yosuke Hirayama, 'Late Home Ownership and Social Re-stratification', *Economy and Society* Volume 47, Issue 2 (2018), 257–79.

Ian Mulheirn, James Browne and Christos Tsoukalis, *Bringing It Home: Raising Home Ownership by Reforming Mortgage Finance*, Tony Blair Institute for Global Change (London: 27 May 2022).

Committee Report: Planning Committee on 9 May 2016, Item No. 4, Case Number 15/4714, Brent Council (9 May 2016).

'Local authority housing statistics data returns for 2020 to 2021', Gov.uk <gov.uk/government/

statistical-data-sets/local-authority-housing-statistics-data-returns-for-2020-to-2021> [accessed 26 April 2022].

Angele Storey and Ngarie Coombs, *Living Longer: implications of housing tenure in later life*, Office for National Statistics (London: 18 March 2020).

Beth Manders and Paul Breen, *Deaths of homeless people in England and Wales: 2020 registrations*, Office for National Statistics (London: December 2021).

Craig Smith, *Housing Affordability in England and Wales: 2021*, Office for National Statistics (London, March 2022).

Ceri Lewis, *UK House Price Index September 2021*, Office for National Statistics (London: 17 November 2021).

Tim Pateman, *Housing Building, UK: permanent dwellings started and completed*, Office for National Statistics (London: 19 January 2021).

Housing Affordability in England and Wales: 2021, Office for National Statistics (London: 23 March 2022).

Overview of the UK Population: January 2021, Office for National Statistics (London: 14 January 2021).

'Population estimates for the UK, England and Wales, Scotland and Northern Ireland statistical bulletins', ons.gov.uk <ons.gov.uk/peoplepopulationandcommunity/populationandmigration/populationestimates/

bulletins/annualmidyearpopulationestimates/
previousReleases> [accessed 26 April 2022].

S. D. Platt, C. J. Martin, S. M. Hunt and C. W. Lewis,
'Damp housing, mould growth, and symptomatic
health state', *BMJ* Volume 298, Issue 6689 (1989),
1673–8.

'Trends in non-decent homes by tenure', *The
Health Foundation*, 19 April 2021 <health.org.uk/
evidence-hub/housing/housing-quality/trends-
in-non-decent-homes-by-tenure> [accessed 3 May
2022].

'SIGOMA analysis reveals how austerity has fallen
disproportionately on urban authorities', SIGOMA
(21 June 2020) <sigoma.gov.uk/news/2020/
sigoma-analysis-reveals-how-austerity-has-
fallen-disproportionately-on-urban-authorities>
[accessed 28 April 2022].

*Table 241: House building: permanent dwellings
completed, by tenure, United Kingdom historical
calendar year series*, Department of Levelling
Up, Housing and Communities and Ministry of
Housing (4 July 2019).

*Table 244: House building: permanent dwellings started
and completed, by tenure, England (historical calendar
year series)*, Department of Levelling Up, Housing
and Communities and Ministry of Housing (10
March 2022).

'Local authority housing statistics data returns for 2020 to 2021', Gov.uk <gov.uk/government/ statistical-data-sets/local-authority-housing- statistics-data-returns-for-2020-to-2021> [accessed 26 April 2022].

Rt Hon Michael Gove MP, 'Government Approach to Building Safety', 10 January 2022.

Rt Hon Michael Gove MP, 'Government Response to Industry Proposal on Building Safety', 7 March 2022.

'Brokenshire unveils new measures to stamp out "poor doors"', Gov.uk (20 July 2019) <gov.uk/ government/news/brokenshire-unveils-new- measures-to-stamp-out-poor-doors> [accessed 28 April 2022].

'Understanding landlords', NatCen, July 2013 <natcen.ac.uk/our-research/research/ understanding-landlords> [accessed 28 April 2022].

'Record number of children and young people referred to mental health services as pandemic takes its toll', Royal College of Psychiatrists, 23 September 2021 <rcpsych.ac.uk/news- and-features/latest-news/detail/2021/09/23/ record-number-of-children-and-young-people- referred-to-mental-health-services-as-pandemic- takes-its-toll> [accessed 28 April 2022].

'Building Better', National Housing Foundation,

<housing.org.uk/buildingbetter> [accessed 3 May 2022].

'Welfare Spending: Universal Credit', Office for Budget Responsibility <obr.uk/forecasts-in-depth/tax-by-tax-spend-by-spend/welfare-spending-universal-credit> [accessed 26 April 2022].

50 years of the English Housing Survey, Department for Communities and Local Government (2017) <assets.publishing.service.gov.uk/government/uploads/system/uploads/attachment_data/file/461439/EHS_Households_2013-14.pdf>.

'Locata Housing Options', Brent Council <legacy.brent.gov.uk/media/16410210/locata-housing-options-page.pdf> [accessed 25 April 2022].

'About homelessness', Crisis <crisis.org.uk/ending-homelessness/about-homelessness> [accessed 28 April 2022].

Guidance on the Financial Policy Committee's recommendation on loan to income ratios in mortgage lending, Financial Conduct Authority (London: August 2014).

'House Building in England', Fullfact.org (28 March 2018) <fullfact.org/economy/house-building-england> [accessed 26 April 2022].

Gemma Kappala-Ramsamy, 'Statement on the lifting of the council housing borrowing cap', Londoncouncils.gov.uk (3 October 2018)

<londoncouncils.gov.uk/node/34487> [accessed 3 May 2022].

Abdool Kara, 'Local government in 2019: a pivotal year', NAO blog (13 February 2019) <nao.org.uk/naoblog/local-government-in-2019> [accessed 28 April 2022].

Adam Corlett and Felicia Odamtten, 'Hope to buy: The decline of youth home ownership', Resolution Foundation, December 2021.

Journalism, Articles and Other Resources

Paul Boateng, 1987 Maiden Speech in the House of Commons <ukpol.co.uk/paul-boateng-1987-maiden-speech-in-the-house-of-commons>, <group.legalandgeneral.com/media/cxihcr20/bomad-under-35s_final-1.pdf> [accessed 28 April 2022].

'Bank of Mum and Dad funds one in two house purchases among under-35s Legal & General research reveals', Legal & General Group Plc, October 2021.

'Unsafe cladding: What is it and who pays to remove it?' BBC News, 13 April 2022 <bbc.co.uk/news/explainers-56015129> [accessed 28 April 2022].

Andy Beckett, 'The right to buy: the housing crisis that Thatcher built', *Guardian*, 26 August 2015 <theguardian.com/society/2015/aug/26/

right-to-buy-margaret-thatcher-david-cameron-housing-crisis> [accessed 26 April 2022].

'Lacking a fixed address or a safe place to receive mail will worsen Covid hardships, warns Citizens Advice', Citizens Advice, 24 September 2022 <citizensadvice.org.uk/about-us/about-us1/media/press-releases/lacking-a-fixed-address-or-a-safe-place-to-receive-mail-will-worsen-covid-hardships-warns-citizens-advice> [accessed 28 April 2022].

Coliving.com <coliving.com> [accessed 3 May 2022].

'Pandora papers: biggest ever leak of offshore data exposes financial secrets of rich and powerful', *Guardian*, 3 October 2021 <theguardian.com/news/2021/oct/03/pandora-papers-biggest-ever-leak-of-offshore-data-exposes-financial-secrets-of-rich-and-powerful> [accessed 28 April 2022].

'Pandora Papers', International Consortium of Investigative Journalists <icij.org/investigations/pandora-papers> [accessed 28 April 2022].

Harriet Grant and Chris Michael, 'Too poor to play: children in social housing blocked from communal playground', *Guardian*, 25 March 2019 <theguardian.com/cities/2019/mar/25/too-poor-to-play-children-in-social-housing-

blocked-from-communal-playground> [accessed 28 April 2022].

'Mr Peabody's Gift', *The Times*, 1 February 1864.

John Harris, 'The end of council housing', *Guardian*, 4 January 2016 <theguardian.com/society/2016/jan/04/end-of-council-housing-bill-secure-tenancies-pay-to-stay> [accessed 26 April 2022].

Lorraine King, 'New homes bid for former council building in Wembley sold for almost £10m', *Brent & Kilburn Times*, 13 July 2015 <kilburntimes.co.uk/news/new-homes-bid-for-former-council-building-in-wembley-sold-3737554> [accessed 25 April 2022].

'Property valuation: Mahatma Gandhi House, 34 Wembley Hill Road, Wembley, Brent, Greater London, HA9 8AD', The Move Market <themovemarket.com/tools/propertyprices/mahatma-gandhi-house-34-wembley-hill-road-wembley-ha9-8ad> [accessed 3 May 2022].

'Mahatma Gandhi House', Mayor of London / London Assembly <london.gov.uk/what-we-do/planning/planning-applications-and-decisions/planning-application-search/mahatma-gandhi-house> [accessed 3 May 2022].

Larry Elliott, 'A brief history of British housing', *Guardian*, 24 May 2014 <theguardian.com/business/2014/may/24/history-british-housing-decade> [accessed 26 April 2022].

Semayne's case (1604), All ER Rep 62.

'Letting agent fees for tenants', Shelter <england.shelter.org.uk/housing_advice/private_renting/letting_agent_fees_for_tenants> [accessed 28 April 2022].

'The story of social housing', Shelter <england.shelter.org.uk/support_us/campaigns/story_of_social_housing> [accessed 26 April 2022].

Catherine Philp and Chris Smyth, 'Ukraine crisis: US sounds alarm over Russian "dirty money" in London', *The Times*, 28 January 2022 <thetimes.co.uk/article/ukraine-crisis-us-sounds-alarm-over-russian-dirty-money-in-london-xrwfrhw57> [accessed 3 May 2022].

Michael Savage, 'Millennial housing crisis engulfs Britain', *Observer*, 28 April 2021 <theguardian.com/society/2018/apr/28/proportion-home-owners-halves-millennials> [accessed 28 April 2022].

ABOUT THE AUTHOR

Hashi Mohamed arrived in Britain as a child refugee, and is now a barrister at No5 Chambers in London, where he specialises in planning and environment law, with a specific focus on housing. A contributor to the *Guardian*, *The Times* and *Prospect*, he is also a contributing editor at Tortoise Media and regularly presents documentaries for BBC Radio 4, most recently on the housing crisis. His first book, *People Like Us*, looked at social mobility and inequality and was a Radio 4 Book of the Week. Hashi is a board member of the Coin Street Secondary Housing Co-operative, a member of the Chartered Institute of Housing and a trustee of the Big Education Trust.